21
SECRETS
OF
REAL ESTATE
MILLIONAIRES

———————◆———————

AS REVEALED BY THEIR ATTORNEY

Jay W. Mitton, MBA, JD

Foreword by
William D. Danko, PhD
Co-author, *The Millionaire Next Door*

For further information, contact: 800-837-9093
If no answer, call: 800-748-5223
Web Site: NationalRealEstateInvestors.com

Second Edition
First Printing 2004

Library of Congress Cataloging-in-Publication Data

Mitton, Jay W., 1941—

21 Secrets of Real Estate Millionaires, As Revealed by Their Attorney, Jay W. Mitton, MBA, JD

ISBN: 1-928845-32-0

Printed in the United States of America

10   9   8   7   6   5   4   3   2   1

A WORD FROM THE AUTHOR

It has been my privilege to spend my entire professional energies learning and teaching the art of asset and lawsuit protection. As an attorney, I have been the legal advisor to many of the most gifted financial minds of our times. As I designed my clients' advanced tax planning and asset protection portfolios, they often shared with me how they had made their fortunes.

Someone once said that the quickest way to become a millionaire is to be mentored by a millionaire. I shall be forever grateful to my clients for sharing their personal tips and money-making strategies with me. I now feel a personal responsibility, even a privilege, to share these marvelous insider secrets with my friends, associates, and others who might benefit.

It was Francis Wayland who said: "Wealth is not acquired, as many persons suppose, by fortunate speculations and splendid enterprises, but the daily practice of industry, frugality, and economy."

The real estate investment secrets contained in this book are my way to *give back* to America. I have been mentored by the best, as they have cast their bread on the waters of wealth accumulation. In writing this book, I am making an effort to return the kindness extended me by others. In this spirit, I have decided to not only share what I have learned, but also to donate royalties from the sale of this book to charity.

It is my hope that the following pages will be an exciting journey of discovery for you. I truly believe it is the most comprehensive book ever written on creating real estate wealth. The ideas came from clients who are millionaires and multi-millionaires. THEY DID IT, and so can you.

Jay W. Mitton, MBA, JD

FOREWORD

by
WILLIAM D. DANKO, PhD
Coauthor, *The Millionaire Next Door*

Little did I know when *The Millionaire Next Door* was published in 1996, that it would sell more than two-million copies. It created previously unimagined opportunities for me, a marketing educator. Where I teach, at the State University of New York at Albany, I thoroughly enjoy working with students in a traditional sense, acquiring and passing on marketing knowledge. The book I published serves as a lightning rod of sorts, attracting a massive external public that seeks me out to share their experiences. No matter which source of students, I am enriched because I continue to learn.

One of the most influential "students" I have the pleasure of working with is Jay Mitton, the widely acclaimed "father of asset protection." My own studies on the affluent are consistent with the theme he addresses in this book: real estate is a vital element in every well-diversified portfolio. Now, after a lifetime of acquiring detailed knowledge on this topic, Jay is ready to share the *21 Secrets of Real Estate Millionaires*.

Several characteristics make this book unique. Over his professional career, Jay has learned how various investing strategies have helped his clients become real estate millionaires. These clients have shown Jay the strategies and tactics that focus on acquisition and disposal of properties — at a profit! He also learned that this process is not a random event. It is based on clear principles executed with discipline, again reaffirmed by his clients. Not only has Jay learned vital lessons from others, he has also personally implemented them as well.

It is clear that Jay wrote this book to unselfishly share what he has learned . . . to "pass it on." It is written from the vantage point that anyone serious about success with real estate will seek out and utilize the direction that only a qualified trainer/coach/mentor can give. Truly, Jay Mitton is an individual who has much to offer each of us. Hopefully, future students will internalize the important lessons found here, thereby creating yet another generation of real estate millionaires.

William D. Danko, PhD

CONTENTS

SECTION III:

FINE-TUNING YOUR REAL ESTATE INVESTMENT BUSINESS

DEDICATION

I wish to thank those who have assisted me in the writing of this book. These include my secretary, Barbara Munson, and my associates James M. Smith and Nathan Brown. W. Emerson Brantley III and Brenton G. Yorgason assisted in the forming of the book, and editors Cara O'Sullivan, Lisa Crockett, and Richard Peterson labored tirelessly in their efforts.

Finally, I express my appreciation to my partners, James J. Mitton and Mitchell B. Huhem, and my wife, Joan. Their support and encouragement have been invaluable.

ACQUIRING THE INVESTOR MIND-SET

❖

*The Foundational Strategies for
Real Estate Investing*

1

CAPTURING YOUR DREAMS

———————◆———————

As the person introducing me began to talk, I again felt a tinge of embarrassment. I was about to speak to over 22,000 people gathered at the Reunion Arena in Dallas, Texas. Excitement suddenly swelled within me as the master of ceremony's introduction came clearly through the loudspeaker:

"We now have a real treat for you. Our next speaker, in his area of specialty, has taught more people and has been on more television and radio talk shows than anybody in history. He is known as the father of asset protection. A prominent attorney, newspaper columnist, and best-selling author, he is recognized as the number one authority in America on lawsuit and asset protection."

Expecting the introduction to conclude, I was surprised as he continued: "Ladies and gentlemen, you may be surprised by what this speaker is going to tell you. You may expect his excitement to be about the subject for which he is internationally renown — asset protection. That is only part of it. The most electrifying part will be the rest of his story. Today we have asked Mr. Mitton to also tell us how his wealthy clients became millionaires."

I quickly took the microphone and began my remarks:

"Good morning, ladies and gentlemen. I appreciate the opportunity to speak with you today. In addition to my normal subject, I have been asked to share the secrets of how millionaires create wealth. Whether it is the first million, the tenth million, or the first billion, they all say the same thing — that the way to become wealthy in America today is in real estate. In fact, other than one exception — a man who became wealthy buying the right stocks — every client I've known, who has reached the multi-millionaire and mega-millionaire status, has done so by investing in real estate.

"I've always thought it a paradox that clients would pay me to learn how to protect their assets, while at the same time sharing with me how to create wealth for my own family. In reality, I was paid twice for my efforts.

"Realizing that real estate is the primary arena in which to create wealth, I began to learn the various real estate strategies of my millionaire clients. After years of searching and learning, I identified twenty-one successful approaches to real estate investing. This doesn't mean that each of my clients used all of these strategies. Most of them used between one and five of them.

"When I realized this, I concluded that creating wealth is accomplished through a two-step process. The first step is to gain a comprehensive understanding of all twenty-one strategies. The second step is to narrow the real estate investment approaches to a small number of these, then focus efforts on the chosen few.

"As I implemented my own wealth-enhancing strategies, I restricted my areas of involvement. Rather than trying to implement all of the strategies, I reduced my approaches to include only those I could easily manage. This resulted in my becoming an expert in five of the twenty-one real estate strategies.

"Permit me to speak personally for a moment. When I was a small boy, I lived in very austere conditions. Even though our family had very little money, my mother taught us to make sugar cookies. Using small preformed strips of metal, we shaped all sorts of animal figures. We literally used cookie cutters, with which we formed our cookie dough. The phrase 'cookie cutters' took on a very definite meaning.

"Through my millionaire clients, I have found twenty-one strategies — cookie cutters, if you will — that they used to create wealth in real estate. These strategies were so basic that I implemented several of them in my own business life. I then taught two of these strategies to my son, James. He listened closely, and in just a few short months he was on his own road to becoming wealthy."

The next sixty minutes were a blur. Never, in the thousands of times I had spoken on legal topics, had my audience seemed so animated. As they learned the insider secrets of real estate millionaires, they seemed to thirst for more. Without question, I had found the "hot button" of thousands of future millionaires!

Soon I was flying home. As the plane droned into the growing darkness of the night, my thoughts turned to one of my real estate investor friends, James Smith. I had met him months earlier, and had been deeply impressed. He had a commanding presence, he was articulate, and he was honest. Married for twenty-five years and the father of two college-age sons, he was a man of strong character.

Weeks earlier, when I asked James to share with me his premillionaire beginnings, I could never have anticipated his response. "To be perfectly honest," he began, smiling, "no one really gave me much of a chance. I have been dyslexic since birth, and my high school counselor cautioned me against dreaming of more than an average lifestyle. My grades were at the bottom of my high school graduating class, and I was doomed to a life of mediocrity.

"But, was I really? Once I finished school, I was mentored by a friend who understood real estate investments. After cautioning me against adopting a 'get rich quick' mentality, he proceeded to teach me how to buy my first piece of property.

"I rolled up my sleeves, then spent three days before my high school graduation looking at properties. Using my friend's formula, I purchased a small house. I later sold it, made several thousand dollars profit, and was on my way."

James continued with his story. "By the time I had thrust both feet into the real estate investment waters, I was hooked. The more I immersed myself, the more I realized that it was the perfect business for me to be in. It was conservative, I began to make money in large lump sums, and the tax benefits were huge. Even more important, I soon learned that each real estate purchase was an addition to my own self-directed retirement program. I sensed that if I remained conservative, I would have unlimited income potential. Even more important, my monthly cash flow would more than adequately care for my needs. In short, I began to accumulate, fix up, then resell properties.

"About this time, my mother was in her late fifties. She had taught third grade for over thirty years and was preparing to retire on $1,800 per month. When I explained my real estate investing formula to her, she determined to jump right in. Within a short period of time, she had purchased twelve pieces of property. Her monthly positive cash flow exceeded $10,000. With no debt, she has been able to spend the last two decades traveling and enjoying life to her heart's content — and all because she began to let money work for her, instead of working for her money."

REAL ESTATE – THE AMERICAN DREAM

James and his mother are living the American dream. While their story is by no means unique, it is illustrative of the wealth any American can achieve. What *is* unique is the comprehensive success formula James developed in amassing his fortune. He acquired a thorough understanding of effective real estate investment cookie cutters.

It is no wonder that real estate has been called the "universal business." Every day tens of thousands of homes are bought, sold, built, or renovated. People move in, they move out, and they move on. They buy, sell, rent, and lease. Some of these home owners make money, some are foreclosed on; some build equity, others spend years paying rent. Sadly, my misguided uncle was one of these. He recently passed away, effectively bankrupt, leaving my aunt with little means of support. He believed that a person should always rent, never own. He was a good man, but held an erroneous philosophy.

From our youth, most of us dream of owning our own home. As children, we play house, we build tree houses, campsites, and forts. As teens, we count the days until we can move into an apartment of our own. We struggle through apartments, roommates, moves with friends, new jobs, new romances, then marriage. Finally, one day we buy our own home.

No wonder the idea of buying real estate is such a mental and emotional mountain to climb. It is a wonder that any of us break free from our deeply held beliefs and learn to actually *use* real estate to make a dramatic financial difference in our life.

WHY REAL ESTATE?

Perhaps you are wondering, as did I, why real estate is so *good*, why it is better than almost any other business for amassing wealth. I owned a successful legal practice and although I was not a greedy person, deep down I was aware that money, or the lack of it, had great power over my life.

Even more specifically, I knew that the hours in my day were limited. I only had a certain number of hours to spend with a limited number of clients. I could add partners, staff, spend more advertising dollars, and add additional overhead and stress. But, like a doctor in his practice, there was a ceiling on my income potential, based on the hours in my day.

Your income is generally limited to the number of hours you can trade each day for money. Real estate investing has no such capstone. Your potential income and wealth creation is unlimited.

During the early hours of my financial discovery, I believed that it took money to make money. Thus, I began to leverage my money to make it work for me. I distinctly remember a conversation I had with myself one day. I figured that if I invested $5,000 with my stock broker, then saw an increase of ten percent, I would only earn $500. I realized that at this rate it would take me years to reach my financial goals. I remember thinking, *I wish I could reach a point where I could leverage the hours of my life, instead of trading them for my 'daily bread,' where I could make money day in and day out, and have more time to enjoy with my family.*

This is exactly what I found real estate investments can provide. I began to understand the principle of *leveraging*, and how I could leverage my money and my time through the correct use of real estate.

Using the same formula as above, I could follow the example of my millionaire clients. I could invest $5,000 in real estate, and often control a piece of property worth $250,000 or more. I learned that when this $250,000 property increased ten percent, my investment earned $25,000. This was five times my original investment, or a 500 percent return. *That* was leverage! On one occasion, one of my multi-millionaire clients said to me, "I owe my entire fortune to my understanding of leverage."

Before continuing, let me be clear in stating that my purpose is not to discount the value of stocks, bonds, and other investments. We should all strive to have a balanced, diversified investment portfolio. Still, nothing I have found compares with real estate in providing return on investment. Nothing I have found gives as much leverage. This is why more millionaires make their money in real estate than through any other investment vehicle.

The good news is that you too can join their ranks. In fact, every sixty seconds a new millionaire is created. Beginning today, you can become one of them — a true multimillionaire. (Not coincidentally, 12,000 people move their residence every sixty seconds. No wonder real estate is the answer!)

The advantage of real estate investing goes far beyond the remarkable rate of return on your dollars.

Additional Advantages Include the Following:

1. You can build a lucrative monthly cash flow today and a retirement income for your future.

2. It does not take money to make money, yet you can make thousands of dollars (or tens, or hundreds of thousands) on each transaction.

3. You get significant tax advantages, such as depreciation. This occurs even though real estate typically appreciates by growing in value.

4. Appreciation also makes real estate the greatest means of preserving your wealth.

5. You are not locked into one place of residence. You can invest in real estate from anywhere in the country.

6. You can build a small or large business, and do this in addition to what you are already doing.

The secret of becoming a millionaire is this: Real power comes when you move beyond the "do-it-yourself" realm into the arena of true success. This occurs when you take it upon yourself to seek out and learn from an experienced mentor who will personally guide and train you.

May I suggest that you begin your journey by picking one or two of the "cookie cutters" found in this book. You will be amazed at how quickly your wealth will begin to accumulate.

The day I began writing this chapter, I took an unemployed handyman under my wing and taught him one of my favorite cookie cutters. The two of us even selected his first real estate investment. I am convinced he is on his way to becoming a millionaire, and so can you. Please read on!

2

HOUSES AND HOMES:
SEEING THROUGH THE EYES
OF AN INVESTOR

———————◆———————

OF HOUSES AND HOMES

As you read this book, I am going to ask you to do something difficult. I invite you to stop thinking of houses as being unique. Sentimentally thinking of a house as a "Cute three-bedroom, two-bath ranch style, with family room, central heat and air, new roof," or "Perfect for first-time homeowners, near good schools and parks," is only part of the problem. Real estate agents, like most people in sales, understand the psychological effect that descriptions like these have on a client's emotions. Agents know that buying a home is an emotional experience for most buyers, and nothing is more emotional than the idea of a warm hearth, a safe haven from the world outside, a happy home.

Try to detach yourself emotionally from your "dream" home, your first home, or the home in which you grew up. Begin to envision a house the way an investor would. Think of a home as a money-making "house." Look beyond the beautiful music playing in the background of the house you are imagining. Also ignore the sweet aroma of bread baking in the oven. Ignore the beautiful furniture a real estate agent has loaned the house seller to induce you to buy based on emotions.

Houses are what you buy and sell. Your "home" is where you live, where your family resides, and where your heart is. There is a big difference in the two.

While we many never consciously think about it, most people are aware of only one kind of price for a house: retail. When we see signs for new houses that say, "Houses from the $150s," we immediately think that the only differences are how many bedrooms or baths, or which floor plan is chosen. We all know there is some room to negotiate, but how much wiggle room is there? The concept of buying houses at wholesale prices conjures up some millionaire assistant with checkbook in hand, paying cash to a desperate new widow for her home — at below market price.

This tragic misconception has kept more people out of wholesale real estate investing than any other.

So much for the "new house" concept. Think for a moment about all the existing houses in your area. Streets of houses, neighborhoods of houses, urban and suburban, houses on this side of town or that side of town. Houses in your part of the state, in your region of the country. Millions of houses everywhere.

A Vast Generic Market:
The "Used-house" Market

Every day, thousands of houses are being bought and sold at all kinds of prices and for all kinds of reasons. People are moving, divorcing, marrying, retiring, graduating, relocating, being born, and dying. Money is changing hands — hundreds of millions of dollars everyday.

Whenever you have a huge market of physical goods changing hands daily, the "products" can be bought (or sold) as unique-branded goods, or they can be handled as generic products that are part of a massive, homogenous group. The group as a whole forms a market. The individual item is just one of millions.

When you think of nuts and bolts, do you only buy one unique brand, or do you consider all nuts and bolts as generic? Chances are, you have never given this much thought. Do you buy a certain brand of hamburger, or whatever your local fast-food business produces? A new car dealer usually is identified with one or two "brands," while a used-car dealer is just a car dealer. He does not think of the cars on his car lot as part of a neighborhood. Instead, they are his inventory. I'm sure you get the picture.

Houses are generic products, bought and sold at prices that can range from pennies on the dollar, to wholesale, to "distributor" pricing, to retail, to more than retail — whatever the market will bear.

This may sound cold and jar your senses, but for just a few minutes take the emotional hook of "home" out of your equation. When a stock investor has a chance to sell at a substantial profit, do you think he or she becomes bogged down in, "I cannot sell this stock. My grandfather worked there." The stock gets sold anyway. Why? Because the stock is only a piece of paper — an investment to be held until a person can cash it in and earn a return on his or her investment.

Houses are part of a vast, homogeneous market that are bought, sold, and traded in huge numbers every day. They may be unique on an individual basis, but as an investor, you are dealing with them only as a product.

To a real estate investor, houses are impersonal commodities to be bought for the purpose of making money. They are rented, leased, or sold when the opportunity presents itself for a calculated return on investment.

How to use it: Completely stop thinking in terms of "home." Think "house, building, product, or inventory." A house is not a home until your buyers close on it, moves in, and makes it their little piece of heaven.

Taking the sentimental feelings out of the picture is a prerequisite to building a successful real estate investing business. As you begin to look at the houses in your area with the understanding that they are your commodities, the products on which you will build your business, they will be seen in a different light.

THE HOUSES AROUND YOU WILL BECOME YOUR INVENTORY.

How you buy and sell this inventory will define your business. There are two basic ways a house can be purchased:

1. *Retail for others*, those who buy to make a dwelling their home or domicile.
2. *Wholesale for you*, as a real estate investor.

In summary, this brief chapter has been presented with the aim of having you detach yourself from the personal nature of buying real estate. Live in your home, but invest in houses. Think of your purchases as money in the bank, to be withdrawn when each house is sold. With this millionaire mind-set, you are well on your way to setting up your real estate money-making business.

3

RUNNING YOUR BUSINESS
LIKE A BUSINESS

◆

Before considering the foundational strategies for specific types of deals, let's examine how you think about your business, and how integrally this mind-set is linked to your success. If you consider your business casually — as a side business for extra money — you are missing the boat. This is true whether you spend two or three hours a week, or work at it full time. The attitude that succeeds is the attitude that this is a viable business and one that should be treated with the same importance as any other business.

If you treat real estate investments as a little business *or* a big business, either way you will get what you expect.

BASIC COMMON-SENSE DISCIPLINE

Block your time. If you plan to spend three hours a week on your real estate business, schedule your three hours and *block the hours on your calendar*. If you scheduled a staff meeting on Thursday mornings each week, would you sometimes show up and sometimes sleep in? I'm sure you wouldn't. Why would anyone ever consider the time spent in their real estate investment business less important than the hours of their life they dedicate to someone else's business or to their job?

Establish a work area. Set aside a place to work that is exclusively used for your real estate business. No recipe cards or sewing machines, no beds or power tools, no toy boxes or games. Clear the decks! This is your financial future, and it is worth it.

INCORPORATE PROFESSIONAL HYGIENE

Blocking your time and establishing an exclusive work area combine to fashion what I refer to as *professional hygiene.* Professionals who are hygienic in their approach will accomplish more, and will do so with less stress and clutter than they otherwise would have done. It is the only way in which to conduct business.

GIVE YOURSELF THE PROPER TOOLS

Other than your training, the following are specific tools you need to facilitate your business growth:

1. **A telephone.** Rather than put in a second business line, I recommend purchasing a cellular phone. Why? It is invaluable to have a phone when you are looking at houses, when you need to call a seller or lender, or when you are running late (or early) for an appointment. Plus, having a phone with you gives you the opportunity to confer with your personal coach or advisor while you are actually looking at a physical property, so that you can strategize while "on location."

2. **A calendar, planner, or PDA.** Carry this with you at all times. I personally prefer a standard planner, but a personal digital assistant (PDA) device works just as

well. Managing your time is an absolute necessity to make your efforts more efficient and effective. It creates a mind-set that says, "I do not have time to waste. My time is money!" If you have a problem managing your time, check with your local business association, Chamber of Commerce, or college, and take a class on the subject.

3. **Install a bulletin board, chalk board, or white board.** This will help you keep up with your deals and offers. Or, if you have a computer, use a good tracking software to keep track of the deals and the prospective buyers and sellers that your successful business will generate. Choose one custom-designed for real estate investors to provide exactly the kind of tracking you need in your business.

4. **Purchase a computer with a modem and printer.** If you do not have a computer, you need one. It may be quaint to say you do not have one, and you could probably get by without one. But why handicap yourself when new computers are relatively inexpensive? You will find it invaluable for putting together letters, flyers, and contracts, not to mention going online to find tax records, foreclosures, and being able to e-mail your advisor, lenders, buyers and sellers. The list goes on and on. A computer in this business will pay for itself a thousand times over.

   If you cannot afford a computer at this time, do not let this stop you from doing business. Initially, you can go online at most public libraries to get property information. You can also use computers and printers at various office services boutiques. As soon as you close your first deal, however, bite the bullet and come into a new world by purchasing a computer. You will forever be thankful you did.

When you acquire your computer, make sure it comes with a modem or that you have some other Internet access available. This is important for faxing and e-mailing, as well as for checking public records online. If you already have an older computer, I would suggest you go ahead and get a new laptop, one you can take with you and access your files and other information while in the field. You will also want a printer, so you can print out your forms and reports, as well as your own cards and letters.

5. **Software.** There is good software for any purpose, but make sure you get tracking and scheduling software. Get one that has been designed by real estate investors for your kind of business. This software is invaluable to assist you in staying on top of your business.

6. **Fax machine.** With a computer and a modem, not only can you go online and e-mail, you can also send and receive fax messages. These faxed messages will come right to your e-mail account. For a small fee, you can also fax out documents.

7. **Financial calculator**. Having a calculator will become increasingly important in your business. As you grow in the advanced strategies found in Section II of this book, there will be times when you will want to utilize a financial calculator. In fact, you will learn techniques that you can put to use as you are doing the foundational strategies as well.

8. **Business cards and letterhead.** These basic items are needed in your business. The good news is that today, with your computer and printer, you can print your own inexpensive cards and stationery that have your contact information for buyers, sellers, and lenders' records.

Now that we have covered some of the tools of the real estate investor trade, let us discuss how you can use these tools to keep your schedule full of profitable deals.

4

No Money Down Deals
Fact, or Fiction

◆

Little Or No Money Down Deals
Yes, You Truly *Can* Find Them

History is replete with real estate deals consummated with little or no money down. One of the most intriguing of these took place on 17 March 1775. On that date, the Transylvania Land Company exchanged $50,000 worth of trading supplies with three Cherokee chiefs. In return, this company was granted all the wilderness embraced by the Cumberland, Ohio, and Kentucky Rivers. It was a good deal for the Cherokee nation, and an even better deal for the land company. No cash was involved.

In this instance and others, much is made of no-money-down deals. From furniture to cars to real estate, we are constantly bombarded with ads touting "no money down." Even so, do you really believe you can buy a house in today's market with no money down? Yes, you truly can. One of my clients, Robert Allen, wrote the classic real estate book, "Nothing Down." He personally shared with me how he and others actually made their acquisitions. Theirs is a bona fide approach to real estate investing and does work.

Buying real estate parcels with no money down is not only possible; it is wise. To be a successful investor, you need several ingredients stirred into your wealth-enhancing approach. These include (a) a creative imagination, (b) personal and professional credibility born of integrity, (c) a sensitivity to the seller's needs, (d) a degree of wisdom to accompany your thoughtful analysis of a given deal, and (e) a willingness to take an educated risk. These ingredients should be considered one at a time.

A creative imagination. Every self-made millionaire I know has been able to think "out of the box." That is, he or she has been able to think beyond the routine way of structuring a deal. In real estate, the environment in which to do this is endless. When a seller is motivated, and their need is firmly established, as a wise and creative investor, you can put all of the elements of the deal together. There is no end to the possibilities of *how* you structure a deal; and the more creative you become, the more successful you will be in accumulating wealth.

Personal and professional integrity. Perhaps this ingredient is the most important of all. There are so many dishonest people doing business that they have created an environment of mistrust. Even so, I have found that a person's reputation precedes them. If you want to do more than one deal in a given community or area, you will do well to establish a reputation for yourself. It must flow from your personal life, and how you conduct yourself, into your business dealings. The most successful millionaires I know believe in Stephen R. Covey's concept of having "win/win" relationships. If you are as concerned for the seller (and their needs) as you are your own, you will become one who is trusted and respected. From my own experience and observation, it is the best calling card in the world.

Being sensitive to the needs of the seller. This concept feeds into the previous statement. Still, it stands alone as an essential ingredient to amassing wealth. It involves the principle of *empathy*. Having empathy is having the ability to put yourself in someone else's shoes. In this instance, it is you, the investor, putting yourself into the shoes of the seller. If he or she can see that you understand their position and that your objective is to help them solve their problems (or liquidate their real estate, or what have you), they will *want* to do business with you.

A thoughtful, wise approach to each real estate purchase. While many good deals must be acted on at once (the early bird therefore getting the worm), no deal should be made without a thorough, methodical approach to making an offer to purchase. Knowledge is the accumulation of facts (in this case *real estate* facts).

Wisdom, on the other hand, is the ability to sift through those facts and make a decision that will bear long-term fruit. When starting out, you may feel a need to rely upon the judgment of others who are more seasoned in the market than are you. It is wise to acknowledge your limited knowledge. As you become more and more seasoned, however, you will instinctively *know* when a deal is good. The important thing, especially in the beginning, is to take the time to consider all options and variables in a given deal.

A willingness to take an educated risk. Our nation's economy is based on what is called the *entrepreneurial spirit.* This is the willingness people have to take a chance. It is only with this attitude of willingness that innovative real estate transactions are designed and implemented. In the professional sports arena, Tiger Woods epitomizes the risk-taker. Still, he does not do this willy-nilly. Every shot he takes is an educated one, and is born of repeated, up-close involvement in his gold "business." From my experience, the most successful real estate investors are those who make the same effort, and of course take the same level of educated risks.

Define what constitutes "money down" or a down payment on a specific property.

Money given to the seller as earnest money. This is totally negotiable and can range from zero to thousands of dollars (Hint: When you buy an investment property, you often stay close to the zero end. When you sell, go for the gusto!)

Earnest money or other real estate contracts bind the contract. Such contracts demonstrate to the seller that you are serious enough about buying their property that they can confidently remove their house from the market. This generally means that even if the sellers are approached by another buyer, they will not sell until you have a chance to finish your purchase in the agreed-upon time.

Do not become extreme about this. Down payment money is no different from the rest of the money in a deal. It all gets counted in the end. It is amazing how many sellers will be satisfied with $500 down or with another modest amount tendered.

The more motivated the seller, the less crossing of the palm with green-backs it takes to get them to agree to your terms. Your contract is a legal document, and putting some small financial binder on it is like a visible "seal" of your intentions. Lawyers call this financial binder "legal consideration."

The difference between the amount the bank will finance and the sales price. If you are financing a property, depending upon your credit worthiness, a bank may approve a small percentage of the purchase price as a down payment. This amount may vary, but can be as low as the required three percent up to ten percent. This amount, along with other miscellaneous closing costs, is the amount of money invested in a given project. Again, you have lots of options here. Sometimes you may find a wholesale house you can put on a credit card. Yes, they can often be purchased this cheaply! Or, the selling price may be low enough and even under the appraised price so that the lender ends up covering all closing costs. They may even cover the down payment if the price is right.

Your share of closing costs. This can include things such as points to the lender, documentary stamps, recording fees, appraisal fees, survey costs, prorated taxes, insurance, and part of the next house payment. Often many of these fees are negotiable between the buyer and seller. Remember: There is no such thing as a "customary" fee that you alone are responsible for.

Everything in a real estate deal is negotiable. Whatever you and the other party agree to, or do not agree to, is entirely up to the two of you. I have personally acquired homes where I agreed to cover closing costs because of a very low purchase price, or I have negotiated closing costs that I knew my buyer would cover. I will share more on this later. Not until you put your signature on the contract does it become binding and unchangeable.

Assumable Loans. Sometimes you still find mortgages and trust deeds that can be assumed without any qualifications required. You can literally give the seller a few hundred dollars moving money and take over the existing loan. Many loans are "assumable" in this way.

In today's real estate environment, most new mortgage loans are either nonassumable, or "assumable with qualifying." Many homes with assumable first mortgages have paid over half their original term, been refinanced at lower interest rates (to get equity out of the house), or have had second mortgage loans added to them. Even so, in many cases you can structure a deal on a house with an older loan, which will allow you to step into the house with little or no money down. The techniques to accomplish this will be discussed later.

Owner-financed. Sometimes an owner has no loan whatsoever, or has already paid off the old mortgage on his house. This may therefore be a dream purchase for you, a real estate investor. You may still be able to make a deal if the seller is motivated enough to do an owner-financed sale. In this deal, the seller becomes your banker. You, in turn, find a buyer who cannot qualify for conventional financing, but one who has saved some down payment (your profit in the deal).   With the ready seller and ready buyer, you have a match made in heaven. There are several ways to make a deal like this work, depending on the house, the existing loan, the seller, and the buyer. If you let your personal advisor walk you through one or two of these options, you will soon find they are a relatively easy source of revenue requiring "no money down." Quite often I have bought homes from sellers who own the property free and clear, but are willing to sell to me for "low or no money down" in order to get a higher interest rate from me than they could get at a bank.

You will also find sellers who want all cash for their

house. Most deals are "all cash" since the seller (or his mortgage company) receives a check at closing. I have never had a single seller ask if the money came from a loan, a credit card, or a bank. It is all cash to them. Likewise, "no money down" can mean several things.

The definition of "No Money Down" is simply this: getting into a house without paying money down. In this type of transaction, the owner either (1) agrees to finance the house, himself, or (2) you as a buyer assume any existing loans on the property. In any case, the seller receives no additional money for their equity. These transactions are the ultimate two no-money-down deals, and I have seen my clients use them often.

Forever put out of your head the notion that you need cash to be in this business. It does not take excessive cash to make money in real estate. "No money down" is real, it works, and there are hundreds of techniques used to accomplish this. It may take a while, but learn as many of these methods as you can. Will every deal be no money down, or limited money down? Certainly not. The key is, you should always assume and expect to do each deal without touching your own money in the process if this is your selected approach to real estate investing. Your job, as a real estate investor, is to collect checks rather than to write them.

How to use it: Even if you have excess cash to use in this business, build it as though you do not. Often an experienced mentor coach can assist you with your first few deals.

What About Your Credit Card Example?

I could hear some mental wheels going "tilt!" when I slipped that in. "Who would ever buy a house on a credit card? After all, the interest would kill you!" And, "Isn't that really paying money down? Even though it is on a card, isn't it real money?"

Credit cards often have a grace period of thirty days or more between statements, and you then have thirty or more days to pay off the balance with zero interest. So, depending on when one uses the card, you often have four to six weeks of free use of the bank's money. I had one client buy six rental homes, using only his several credit cards as the source of the down payments. The key is to have a clear exit strategy before purchasing the property, and whenever possible, to have a ready buyer waiting in the wings to whom you immediately re-sell the property.

The key to doing a no-money-down deal is simple: Structure it so you do not have to take out-of-pocket cash to make it work.

With the guidance of a mentor/trainer or professional advisor, you will find no-money-down deals a powerful way to acquire instant equity in properties with little or no money out of your own pocket.

I observed one of my clients doing it this way: He called on several "For Sale By Owner" ads in his local newspaper. He found that one elderly couple was selling their home in order to free them to get into an elderly care center. My client purchased the house for nothing down, but at full asking price. The sellers were excited to get a note back from the buyer which paid two percent higher interest than they would have received by taking all cash and depositing the proceeds in a low yielding bank savings account. This transaction was a win/win for both parties.

5

BUYING HOUSES WHOLESALE

◆

EVERY PRODUCT HAS A WHOLESALE PRICE

With every product there is a cost to manufacture, a cost to market, a cost to the distributor known as the "wholesaler," and a "retail" cost to the end purchaser. Regardless of the products they offer, that is the basis of all businesses. Even banks buy and sell "paper" loans and credit card debt to other banks at wholesale prices.

Purchasing residential dwellings, "wholesale" does not mean getting several thousand dollars off the asking price. You are looking for deals so good you cannot lose . . . houses for pennies on the dollar. Distress sale houses. Houses you can buy for seventy-five, sixty-five, or even fifty percent less than retail prices of similar, comparable houses. When you buy such properties, the sellers will thank you for taking the house off their hands. Why?

The Wholesale house is always someone's problem. You are offering them an acceptable solution to their problem, freeing them from the responsibility and headaches that have been added to their life. As a real estate investor, you hold solutions in your hand that many owners desperately need.

Having a "Fixer-Upper" Mentality

The term "wholesaling" has reference to buying property that is priced substantially below the market, then re-selling it to another investor generally without fixing it up. Many investors are often too busy or too lazy to locate a suitable fixer-upper on their own. Many investors have back-up buyers in place, then turn the property over to them, realizing a handsome profit. In turn, this buyer will fix up the property, then sell it on the retail market.

A second approach is to buy the property wholesale, then sell it directly on the retail market. This opportunity almost always occurs when an investor has the "fix it" mentality and is acquainted with selling properties, through realtors, on the retail market. One very wealthy widow client uses this strategy almost exclusively. She uses her own crew of remodeling professionals to do the fix-ups.

It goes without saying that buying a fixer-upper occurs when a seller has allowed the property to become run down. It is often not being lived in, the yard is in shambles, and the property as a whole is in disrepair. Or, it may even be in foreclosure with the seller desperate to sell and move.

The investment opportunity with fixer-uppers is substantial. Still, getting involved requires vision. It also requires a blue collar mentality, realizing that additional money and follow-through with sub-contractors will be required to restore the house to its maximum value. This does not mean that you should do the repairs yourself. In fact, often the minute an investor picks up a paint brush, they have begun to use their time unwisely. Good painters can be obtained for twenty-five dollars an hour, and your time is worth many times that. This does not mean that you can't do your own repairs, especially when first starting out.

You may choose to do some of them because you enjoy the "therapy" of doing physical work. In the main, however, keep your time free to find another property. Your ability to quickly enhance your wealth will be easily evident.

Sellers of these properties are looking for someone who can creatively solve their problem. That person may be you.

Think of yourself as a problem solver, and you will open your business to more deals than you can effectively manage. Do not simply be an investor or landlord, or limit yourself to a particular town or area. A friend of mine who owned several businesses over the years actually had this printed on his cards, *"I make problems go away!"*

What a creative and accurate approach. It does not matter if it is in your area or in another part of the country, when considering the purchase of a single-family house, a duplex, or a strip mall, you are looking for a good deal. If you are "only a landlord," you may completely miss a great retail prospect in your own neighborhood. If you only buy single-family houses, you may pass up thousands of dollars profit on the strip mall you might have purchased across town.

How to use it: With experienced guidance, you can develop the attitude and skills that make you a problem-solver. This is someone who makes problems go away for other people. This mind-set removes the limitations from your business potential.

Often the problems you are solving are very unattractive. Face it, if the seller's problems were cute and pretty, their property would already be sold. A "For Sale" property is often a frog, not a prince. Still, your wise efforts in disposing of it will reward you handsomely.

While you can buy distressed situations for far less than comparable houses, the "comp" houses are in good condition, ready for the next family to move in. In real estate investing, we refer to the value of a house's good condition as the "after repaired value." You never buy a wholesale house for anywhere near the retail price. Time and money must be invested in repairs. This is time and money the current owners either do not have or will not invest in their own property. Take heart. You probably won't be spending your time and money doing the fix-ups, either. We will say more about this later.

"A Rose by Any Other Name Would Smell As Sweet"

A "wholesale" house may be called by many names. One of its most common names is a "piece of junk." One of the reasons for this label may be the house's location. It may not be in an area of town you want to spend time in. Then again, it may. As long as it is not located in a high crime area, a drug zone, or a battleground area, it can still work by using several successful methods.

Look to see if other comparable houses in the same area display a degree of pride of ownership. If some of the residents take time to keep their house painted, trim their hedges, and mow their lawns, this is a good sign. As a further caution, do not let the burglar bars keep you away from a bargain. In some areas, crime is normal and accepted.

Where Do You Begin Looking?

Some of the best wholesaling properties are those that are "land-banked." This means that a city or county has actually taken over the property, assuming title for back taxes, etc. While hands-on experience is necessary to know how to purchase land-banked properties, learning this investment vehicle provides a way to quickly build an estate.

Properties are also available when they are red- tagged. This means that a city may tag a house, disallowing it for occupancy until a safety hazard is eliminated. Most municipalities maintain lists of red-tagged properties and will provide a list upon request.

Money Considerations

What is the price target when considering a wholesale purchase of a home? This amount is usually computed to be thirty to fifty percent below the retail market for the home in its forecasted restored state.

When considering purchasing a home in disrepair, you must look beyond the cost of purchase. You must also consider costs of repair and replacement. Discipline yourself to look beyond the obvious eyesore presenting itself. Instead, consider the property's value following restoration.

When you have located a property you are interested in purchasing, construct a cost analysis on the specific items needing repair or replacement. By doing this, you can quickly determine whether or not it is worth buying. These repair items may include unseen problems such as inadequate insulation, heating and air conditioning, electrical, etc. Carpet and padding are also essential to consider, especially if dogs and cats have left their odor.

Plumbing is another item that may not be immediately apparent. Areas such as these need to be closely examined by a professional who can determine existing problems. Color and style of sinks, toilets, tubs, and showers are also critical in calculating resale value.

GETTING IN AND GETTING OUT

One of the primary considerations you must make is the *timing* of your invested cash outlay. That is, how long will your money need to be tied up with a given purchase. Return on investment is the name of the investment game, so you should have the quick-in, quick-out mentality. Turning your money as often as you can maximizes your wealth enhancing opportunities.

When considering the specific areas needing repair, you will do well to remember the axiom, "women buy homes; men don't." Therefore, it is wise to consider what a woman will be looking for in purchasing your investment property. From my experience, they are most often interested in kitchens, bathrooms, and closets.

With these areas in mind, you may need to replace cabinetry. It is often wise to install white sinks and/or toilets. If a home has linoleum or Congoleum flooring, replace it with ceramic tile. Ceramic tile has gone down substantially in cost, and is very much in vogue.

In most regions of the United States, an investor can expect to make a profit of between $15,000 to $25,000 and more per property purchased. This, of course, assumes a standard, moderately-priced home. If you sell the property to turn your dollars, your profit is able to expand into another purchase.

If your strategy is to keep the property and rent it out,

your profit becomes equity based. This may be desirable when your monthly rental cash flow meets your needs. It is common for an investor to get started in the real estate business by turning their property twice in a given year. This often means a $50,000 profit per investment property. Most Americans don't have this much in savings. Investors who have the mentality of "turning" their property, and their money, will often make several million extra dollars by the time they retire.

FEAR PARALYSIS

The worry of getting stuck in a house you can't afford, with repairs you can't make, and a house nobody else wants is one of the biggest fears that hold people back from earning serious money in real estate. It is a fear that can paralyze you and keep you from seeing the underlying value as well as a clear exit strategy with a given property.

A house is only potential quicksand if you 1) forget it is just a commodity, 2) do not properly figure your repairs in advance, or 3) do not have your exit strategy in place from the beginning.

Approach the house as a commodity, and you will not be swayed by a seller's hard-luck story. You will not be persuaded by the condition of the property or by the wonderful home that once was. You will see the house, know its value, figure the required repairs, determine your exit strategy, and know your profit potential before you ever make an offer. The only potential you will look for is the difference between what you can buy the house for, and the amount of profit you anticipate making. And, you will plan this ahead of time!

How to use it: Realize that your applied knowledge will give you the edge over most potential buyers. The understanding and pre-planning of all aspects of the deal ahead of time is the first key to successful deal-making.

One of the ultimate examples of this deal-making technique is the strategy called "simultaneous closing." This is a plan that literally means you are buying and selling the house at the same time. By planning your work and strategically creating a list of ready buyers, you can often have your buyer for the house lined up in advance, before you even make your offer to purchase the house.

Wholesale houses do not have to be unsightly, but such a condition helps. Why? Because a property in disrepair tells you that the owners have not or *could not* care for it. The owners may be 1) strapped for cash, 2) unable physically to maintain their house, 3) being foreclosed on, 4) live out of town, or 5) saddled with a house they have no interest in, as often happens in an estate sale. Each of these circumstances may combine to create the criteria that makes a very successful real estate deal possible for you.

THE MOTIVATED SELLER

In a wholesale house purchase, the seller must have some *extraordinary* motivation to sell his house below the comparable value ("comp" value) of similar homes in the area. They do not want it, they do not like it, they are not going to fix it . . . and most of all they want it to go away. Remember my friend's card: "I make problems go away!"

An associate recently told me: "I just signed my first deal today, not even planning on signing any papers. But they were very motivated and said when I got there that the deal needed to be completed at that very moment. Talk about being in the right place at the right time! And, talk about the power of motivated sellers! I would never have believed someone would want to get rid of their house that badly. I am bubbling with excitement but frightened to death at the same time. This is great!"

If sellers do not have their own motivation, don't waste time negotiating with them. Don't get caught up in worrying about missing the deal; move on. Sellers must already have their own motivation. Generally speaking, you can't force sellers to be motivated to sell.

MOVE QUICKLY

While it is important to be sympathetic with the sellers, it is also wise to remember that you are primarily in business to make money. Making money is the one thing that will keep you in business. You may also be able to help your sellers. If a seller is apathetic, angry, resentful, or unable to make a decision about their life, don't waste time. Move on to the next piece of real estate.

The number of offers you make to qualified sellers who are motivated to make a win/win deal will determine your income. Making offers to unmotivated sellers who only want to win, themselves, has limited potential.

One of the most often asked questions is, "How many offers do I have to make?" The simple answer is simple: "As many as it takes!" Let's narrow the number down. In the beginning, you may have to make five or ten offers in order to have one accepted. You will get better and better in negotiating, and some of the early offers will be with properties or sellers that a few months from now you will not likely waste time on. The important thing is to keep focused on what works, plan your work, and then creatively and methodically work your plan.

You can take this notion to the bank: You will only succeed to the degree you are willing to make offers.

Although you can learn everything there is to know about purchasing real estate, and although you understand legal terms and clauses and have the sharpest sales pitch in town, unless you actually go out and make offers, your success will always be in the form of potential.

Getting turned down and learning to take a little heat by actually "doing it," is the best education of all. Don't worry about getting stuck with an offer you made and later have regrets about. My millionaire clients almost always add a single sentence to their offer, which is worth its weight in gold. Write it down and consider using it whenever you make an offer. It is simply: "This offer is subject to approval of buyer's attorney and accountant."

To have more offers accepted, keep making offers. You can make your motivated sellers' dream come true and end up with a house that can be used in several ways to make money. In a wholesale house, it is difficult, if not impossible, to lose money if you remember that the house is a commodity.

In the next chapter we will discuss the many ways to locate great deals, as well as how to find the motivated sellers who make these deals possible. For now, I encourage you to simply get into the offer-making mentality. It is the only way to proceed at the level that will multiply your wealth.

Learn to use *all* the different ways of finding the bargains, and you will never lack for investors looking to buy them from you.

Investors often spend a great deal of time in self-doubt: "Will I be able to find someone to sell the property to, or will I be stuck with it?" The answer is, there are always buyers, especially when you learn how to find bargains. This may sound simplistic, but it is absolutely true.

In conclusion, remember to let the front end take care of the back end. Find bargains to purchase, and the eventual buyers will find you when you are ready to sell. The faster you get a home repaired, the sooner you can move it. The sooner you move it, the sooner you make money to invest in your next property. Time is money, and money is time. The wisest investor uses both of these assets to his advantage, thereby maximizing his profit potential.

6

FINDING MOTIVATED SELLERS QUICKLY & CONSISTENTLY

———————— ✦ ————————

FINDING WHOLESALE HOUSES

Let us examine several ways to locate incredible bargain houses. Often, you can utilize the services of a real estate agent to search through their multiple listing computer. When you do this, you are able to work out methods of payment that do not require up-front fees to them for providing this service.

If you have time, go for a drive and look for empty, unloved houses. Look for boarded-up houses and overgrown yards. This can be accomplished by setting aside time for this, by using your lunch hour, or by doing something as simple as driving a different route to work each day.

Ask the neighbors if they have any information on the house you may be considering, or if they know about the owners. Recently my widowed mother wanted a new place in which to live. We drove to an area in which she had known people in the past. It was an enclave for senior citizens. There were no "For Sale" signs. When we saw a lady watering her lawn, we stopped and asked, "Do you know of any homes in the area that may be for sale?" She replied, "Why, yes, I do. The neighbors across the street and two houses up have a family problem and must move."

We thanked the woman for the information, then knocked on the door she had pointed to. Within two hours, we had purchased the perfect home in the ideal area — with no real estate fees, and for $41,000 below the comparably priced homes in the area.

Months later, three separate neighbors told my mother that she bought the best real estate "deal" they had ever seen. You can imagine how this made my mother feel. She loves the neighborhood and feels good about the home and all that goes with it.

When you have a few prospective houses with no detailed information on the owners, check the public records for the property owners. Write them a simple letter or give them a call and let them know you are interested in the property.

Finding these wholesale houses is not difficult. Believe it or not, these properties are everywhere. While a wholesale house may not have a seller who is motivated, every motivated seller *does* have a house.

Identifying motivated sellers should become the major focus of your business. Learning effective techniques to continuously find these motivated sellers is a prerequisite to successful wholesale and retail purchases.

You should not make an offer until you have a house with a motivated seller. Also, you cannot buy a house until you make an offer. You cannot make money in real estate until you make an offer that gets accepted.

This is where the "rubber meets the road." It is the pass/fail test for anyone interested in making money in real estate. You can create an entire notebook of motivated sellers, but until you look at the house, speak with your advisors, and actually make an offer, you are playing mind games with yourself. This may seem pretty blunt, but I have no effective way to sugarcoat it.

Locating a motivated seller is Step One for any deal. Step Two is making an offer to purchase.

Finding Motivated Sellers Quickly and Consistently

Mastering the techniques of identifying and connecting with motivated sellers will often be the key to succeeding in your investment business. Eliminating wasted time with unmotivated sellers is an important process you must master until doing so becomes second nature to you. Again, do not find the houses and hope the sellers are motivated. Instead, learn to create opportunities for motivated sellers to seek you out.

Learn to *only* work with motivated sellers. You will likely not motivate anyone. They must create their own motivation. Making offers to unmotivated sellers does not count toward your success. Instead, it only consumes your time.

Many investors waste their time by trying to motivate the sellers they meet. It is an easy trap to step into. If a seller is not motivated on their own, you can't ignite this fire within them. When they are motivated, spend whatever time necessary to cultivate options for purchasing.

The clincher is this: You can often lead the seller into revealing what motivates them. Do not expect every seller to lay all their cards on the table, and don't for one minute think that some are simply ambivalent about selling. You can spend months or years, or dozens of deals, learning which are which. With an advisor, and with experience, you will learn to "cut to the chase" and spend your time with the sellers who are motivated to sell.

How to use it: Learn to recognize the signs of the truly motivated sellers versus those who are wasting your time. Learn to work with the motivated ones and quickly discard the unmotivated.

KEEPING A FULL WAITING ROOM

Did you ever enter a doctor's office when there was no one in the waiting room? To be truthful, I have not. Doctors have a staff of assistants who make sure every minute of their day is full. Why? Because their time is valuable. Of even greater significance, so is yours!

Imagine a giant waiting room for your business. One of the key differences between the average investor and the one with the millionaire mind-set is this: Beginning investors tend to follow this sequence: They buy a house, then seek out a buyer. After completing these two steps, they sell the house and begin all over again to look for another property.

As an advanced investor, you will structure your business so that you always have a "waiting room" full of real estate purchases at every stage. These include new prospective deals, offers that need to be followed up on, "thinkers" who need to be regularly called on, deals that are accepted, and those that are waiting to close.

Your waiting room can handle as many deals as you want. There is ample room for many sellers and many buyers. This is your money pipeline. Keeping your waiting room full of motivated sellers is where you want to focus your energies. Like a good doctor, you know how to handle each case. Simply keep them coming through the door. You should develop consistent programs to keep your waiting room full of deals all the time, so when you finish one, you can stick your head in and say the magical word: "Next!"

By keeping a pipeline full of potential deals, you do not become dependent on or waste time with non-performing deals or unmotivated sellers. When you know you have others waiting in the wings, it is much easier to move to the next deal. This gives you a sense of empowerment and confidence that adds incredible strength in your negotiations with buyers and sellers.

There are dozens of ways to find motivated sellers, and you should test different approaches to find those that work best in your market. Develop these techniques into an ongoing system to find and harvest qualified, motivated leads. Use a phone log or effective tracking software to log actual phone calls, noting how the seller learned about you. Put your advertising where it pulls the greatest numbers of responses. Remember, one house can generate enough revenue to cover all your advertising expenses for the next decade.

How do you find motivated sellers? The real answer to this question is to create a system where motivated sellers find you, and do so consistently. Here are a few methods that have proven effective:

Make your message simple, clear, and strong. Do not mince words or try to sound too polished. Say what you mean and mean what you say. Use newspaper ad phrases such as:

"I want to buy your house. Top cash paid, fast closing. Will buy in any area and in any condition!"

Do you want to purchase "their" house? Of course you do, but only if it fits your program and they are motivated to sell. "Top cash" simply means you will pay the very best price you feel you can offer, under the program you feel the house fits best (wholesale, retail, etc.).

It is good to remember the previous discussion about "no money down" and "all cash deals." You will recall that most deals are cash deals, simply because the seller generally walks away with cash at the time of closing. Would you really buy a house that qualified in any area or any condition? Your answer is "Yes." Remember, you want to make the phone ring, and if the seller is motivated, they want to make a deal. If this is not the case, move quickly to the next deal.

Using a simple message, you can utilize a variety of inexpensive yet very effective approaches such as:

Billboards. Some investors have had success throughout the country with well-placed billboards with the same kind of simple message. An investor in our area has put up several billboards that have an even simpler message. It says simply: "We Buy Ugly Houses!" They include their phone number, and pretty soon the calls start coming in. Above all, work hard until you find what works for you.

Fliers. If there are certain areas you are close to, or that you want to focus on, print fliers and pass them out. You can leave them on doorsteps, or even in the hands of passing motorists.

Classified advertisements. You can also take out similarly worded ads in the local weekly "dollar saver" papers. If your city has a daily paper, running a contract classified ad for a month will often put more calls into your hopper than you can handle. Conversely, you should check out the classifieds every day, looking for motivated sellers who need to move their house. Sometimes the ads will even say, "Distressed Seller!" Others will use other urgent phrases like "Must Sell!" or "Sacrifice!" to let you know they want to immediately do business.

Internet. There is a website for every community, in every city, in every market, where you can post your ads. Test an inexpensive ad on their homepage and see what kind of response you get.

Magnetic signs. These signs cost mere dollars for each side of your car. You will be amazed at how many calls this one little idea will net you. People will literally pull you over to get you to look at their house.

Yard signs. These are not just for the yard of your houses. They are great for placing around town, on telephone poles and other strategic places.

Cable or community access television or local real estate channels. Often your cable company has "menu" ads and community television spots whose costs range from free to next-to-nothing. Or, you may have a local access channel that is used for advertising real estate and real estate-related subjects.

GET PROFESSIONAL GUIDANCE

Ask your personal trainer or professional advisors for guidance on other ways to spread the word. These ways may include creative outside-the-box ideas like joint ventures with other businesses in your area, getting called as a guest expert by local television or radio programs, or being asked to speak to local civic and business groups.

Does all this work? Perhaps the following letter written to one of my associates will make my point:

"I am so glad you had shown me multiple approaches to marketing my services. You never know where the motivated sellers are to be found. By having several strategies for getting the word out, that we are in the business of buying houses, we are hopefully able to reach the largest number of these motivated sellers.

"Just yesterday, a young couple called as a result. Their message was, 'It looks as though we might be able to do business.' Thank you again."

Remember, your strategy as an investor is to find the deals, make the offers, purchase the properties, and get your cash out. To do this you can either find the houses with motivated sellers, or you can learn to find the motivated sellers first. As I have said, they *always* come with a house. You simply need to make an offer.

Unfortunately, many would-be investors spend hours worrying about to whom they will sell, instead of having a house to sell. In this business it truly is, "build it (find the bargains) and they (buyers) will come!"

If your vehicle (or your wagon) is your successful, revenue-generating business built on knowledge, quality guidance, and experience, then your "horse" is your ability to find the deals — finding the houses with sellers who are motivated to make a deal with you. Focus on developing this approach, and your real estate business will fall into place.

7

EXIT STRATEGIES FOR THE WHOLESALE/WHOLESALE HOUSE

———————◆———————

When most people think about reselling, they immediately think about selling to an end-user, a homeowner. We will cover that exciting topic of wholesale-retail in the next chapter, and this is a perfectly valid approach. In this chapter, however, we will explore the wholesale/wholesale approach.

It is good to remember that most people live in only one house, so each time you retail a house to a buyer, you have to find another buyer for the next house . . . then another and another. While selling to a retail customer usually requires some fix-up, the house likewise generates a higher selling price and profit. An alternative approach works great and you must know it.

You are not limited to selling to owner-occupants; you can sell to another investor.

What a concept! Where do other investors get their homes to rent or sell? They have their own strategy, interests, and business plan.

SELLING FOR IMMEDIATE PROFIT – THE "QUICK FLIP"

This is an exit strategy often used by real estate millionaires to quickly "turn" the house for rapid cash out. Some have called this "Buy Low, Sell Low." This re-wholesaling process involves selling to another investor, a landlord, or perhaps an investor who is prepared to repair the house, then resell it to an owner-occupant.

"If I sell to another investor, how can there be enough money for both of us to make a profit on the same house?"

The key is to buy the house at the right price. Remember, when speaking of wholesale houses we are not talking about a few hundred dollars off retail price, we are talking substantially discounted, wholesale property.

All investors are bargain hunters, and as you become adept at finding and structuring wholesale house deals, you will soon develop a waiting list of people ready to buy them from you. This is the essence of the "quick flip," getting cash out as quickly as you can and moving on to the next deal. This is an extremely valuable beginning strategy because it immediately puts money in your pocket.

One millionaire client told me how he applied this wholesale/wholesale approach. He purchased a repossessed property from his own bank for $153,000. The fair market value of this property was closer to $195,000. He sold it days later to an investor for $179,000. The investor was happy because he purchased the property below its retail value. He had another investment house less than one block away from my client's "quick flip" house. This was a win/win for both parties.

Quick Flips do NOT mean you will necessarily get rich quick. For some, it may seem like it, when the first deal nets $10,000, $20,000, or more. Success takes focus and hard work. It also takes guidance and time.

Do not be discouraged if it takes several offers to get your first deal, and do not slow down when the first big bucks start coming in. Once you are in this great race, if you break your stride, you will lose your momentum. This is one of the key pitfalls you must avoid.

Why would people break their stride and stop doing the things that earn them money? It seems that if they start seeing money flow into their account, they would want to keep it flowing. For some, these profits are the most they've ever seen at one time, and suddenly they want to stop and enjoy it. Or, they lose their focus. For others, it is the old devil procrastination: "Okay, we've got some cash now. Let's take our time so we can really make money on the next deal."

Other investors get some money in, and they are satisfied because it is more than they thought they would make, more than they conservatively planned on, and they are happy. For them it is time to relax and take a well-deserved vacation.

A good, strong commitment can help you cut through these and other excuses and keep your pace going through your second, third, fourth deal, and more. Stay focused, and you will forever be glad you did.

Why would a millionaire worry about turning a house for quick cash?

In Section II, we will explore this mind-set further. Suffice it to say that in real estate investing, as in all investing, the key is to turn each dollar as many times as possible within a given year. You do this so that your money is *making* money for you constantly. This format compounds your annual return often to fifty percent, 100 percent, 300 percent, and even more.

In reality, as you begin utilizing the strategies in this chapter, you will find that several thousand dollars profit is the LEAST you can expect to make from these lucrative wholesale deals.

Is quick-flipping property legal?

Certainly. To think otherwise would be ludicrous. Turning property quickly is legal in every area of the country. Equally important, it is one of the quickest ways to accumulate wealth.

Do not mistake this strategy for fraudulent deals such as those where unscrupulous investors pay for padded appraisals, turn in bogus documents to banks to get a buyer financed, or take money disingenuously from purchasers who could not or should not be approved on a loan. Reporters are often looking for a label, and have begun calling improper deals of this nature "flipping" houses.

It is a given that I will not teach, advise, or approve of any illegal or unethical practices in buying or selling properties. There are too many hundreds of honest, ethical, and legal ways to invest in real estate.

There is no room for lack of integrity, especially in a business where your integrity is all you have to build your future on. Your good name and reputation will earn you thousands of dollars as a real estate investor because deals will come to you in response to your ethical dealing with buyers and sellers.

There is only one kind of deal that works: win/win. Your business must be built on integrity, not scamming people out of their homes.

How to use it: Make it easy on yourself. Make every deal win/win. One resulting bonus is that your sellers and buyers will send you more business.

Permit me to make this point even more emphatically. I consider this a personal fundamental mission statement, and I invite you to consider it on that level. My most successful millionaire clients will only consider doing a deal if it is a win/win opportunity.

Finding investor-buyers for your wholesale house: First, contact the landlords in the area.

Landlords are usually easy to locate. In a later discussion, we will cover many ways to find them, even when they are not displaying current "For Rent" signs. These professionals have a stake in the area where your property is located. By learning what the different landlord investors are looking for, you can become a supplier for them.

"Why don't landlords just buy the house themselves? Why go through me?"

Landlords are in the business of renting — advertising, qualifying, collecting, repairing, and preparing for the next renter. They are *not* in the business of looking for and making offers on property. Most landlords have a small portfolio of two or three properties. Often they got in the business because they moved and started renting their old house, or they inherited a house and rented it out. They are more likely to waste a couple of hours changing out a toilet than to spend the same amount of time looking for another rental house (Do you remember our "fears" list?).

I have found that landlords love having a savvy investor supply them with suitable houses for their own investment plan, which is to "buy and hold." We will discuss more about this strategy later.

You can find landlords by writing down "For Rent" numbers, by checking property rolls for people who own several houses in a given area, or by attending a local real estate investors' club meeting.

Contacting Other Investors

There are many investors, most of whom have very little formal training in real estate investing. They are hungry for good deals, and if you can show them how they can make their program work with your property, you will have a sale. Their strategies can dovetail nicely into your own. They may be interested in buying, fixing up, and retailing.

As a caution, do not go overboard in sharing all of your knowledge. Some people enjoy puttering around on houses for months at a time. For them, this is a form of therapy. Learn to let your therapy be depositing closing checks, and you will be their best friend.

Other investors may not be as easy to find as landlords, but there are ways to find them as well. The local real estate investors' club is one way; another is through the classified ads. You will find that these investors often respond to a simple "For Sale by Owner" sign in the front yard. They often pride themselves in thinking that they will pay retail if they go through a realtor. Hence, the "For Sale by Owner" sign attracts them like a bear to honey.

"Why don't these investors simply buy the house themselves? Why go through me?"

The focus of these investors is on whatever house they are involved with right now. It can easily become an all-consuming focus. Running to the paint store, fixing the roof, replacing kitchen cabinets . . . and on and on! They have even more reasons than landlords for not going out and finding houses. I have known of cases where a wholesaler purchased a house within a few doors of one of these "fixer-upper" investors, then sold it to him. The eventual buyer never even knew it was on the market.

Landlords and most other investors put their focus on what they do *with* a house, not on finding houses and making offers.

Most investors are more comfortable doing routine tasks than they are in going out and looking for houses, calling on home owners, and negotiating purchases of houses. Since most do not feel they need a personal trainer or self-education materials to keep them on track, they soon get into a comfort zone of periodically getting another house. They then spend a great deal of time "puttering around" in their business. They often mistake motion for progress.

There is a lesson to be learned from both the landlord and the investor examples: You can find many reasons NOT to look for deals. When the day is over, however, your most important activity is finding more houses and making more offers. Do this right and the rest will fall into place with your financial security assured.

Your *activated* intentions will equal your results. Seek and you shall find.

If you are looking for deals, you will find them. When you are looking, deals will come to you. This is a simple concept, but is one that is missed by so many investors. If you are not looking for a deal, you will probably not find one. It is like wanting to win the lottery but not buying a ticket, only the odds are significantly better.

How to use it: Always be on the lookout for deals. They are always out there, but to find one you've got to be ready.

"Once I have a buyer, what do I do with all the other calls on a particular house?"

What a desirable problem! You may not realize it, but you just stumbled onto the reason why you will never lack for ready buyers. This is also part of the process that will allow you to know your exit strategy and profit before you make your offer.

Everyone who responds to an ad is a qualified potential buyer. They may not be qualified to purchase the particular house you presently own, but you know they have an interest in buying at least one property.

As you ask these questions, you will pre-qualify your potential buyers. These callers will become your prospective buyers list.

The following are things you will want to learn regarding a potential buyer's level of interest:

- ✓ Are they looking to buy a house to live in (retail buyer)?
- ✓ Are they looking to buy a house to live in and fix up (sweat equity buyer)?
- ✓ Are they looking to buy a house to rent (landlord)?
- ✓ Are they looking to buy a house to resell (other investors)?
- ✓ Do they only want houses in this area, or are there other areas they are interested in as well?
- ✓ Do they only want houses in this price range or layout (i.e., 3 bedroom, 2 bath), or are they flexible?
- ✓ How many houses do they plan to buy this year?
- ✓ How much readily-available cash do they have to make a purchase?
- ✓ How is their credit and are they pre-approved at a certain bank for a specific amount?

There are additional questions you will need to ask, but you can see the direction from these. You will begin to create a list of different types of buyers with different interests and needs. This buyers list will be very useful as you look at properties, knowing you already have people who are interested in purchasing a house of some type and condition from you.

As a real estate investor, you should *never* make an offer on a house without clearly planning your exit strategy. This strategy includes your anticipated profit *before* you make your offer.

Your buyers list is a major part of this strategy. Confer with your personal advisor or trainer on all of your early deals, and use the tools presented herein so you know what you plan to accomplish before you go into a deal.

All the software and forms in the world can only help you organize the information on each deal and prospective buyer. You have to take the time to look at each deal and plan and create your strategies.

How to use it: Do not let "analysis paralysis" slow you down. Plan your work, and work your plan.

8

EXIT STRATEGIES FOR THE
WHOLESALE/RESALE HOUSE

———————◆———————

SELL TO "SWEAT EQUITY" OWNER/OCCUPANTS

These people are go-getters who want a house and believe the best way to do this is to (1) get a junker below market, (2) put sweat equity into fixing it up, then (3) either continue to live in it or sell it and buy another. This is their strategy, and it seems to work.

Often, these folks know the least about real estate, but are good with their hands. They have a dream with a plan, and I wish them every success. Theirs is the American dream, and they are using their resources and energy to create wealth. You can become one of their best friends, although unlike previous examples, you do not generally get as many repeat sales from these people.

Why wouldn't sweat-equity people just buy their own house? Why go through me?

The simplest answer is *ignorance*. They do not know where to look, what to look for, how to put a deal together, any of the secrets you will learn to make you successful. Of all the buyers we have discussed, these people are numerically the greatest. They are on their own and likely do not even know about a real estate investor group. Most likely they have been saving their own money to sink into a house and anticipate doing their own repairs to "save money." In addition, most of these buyers do not have a trainer or professional advisor to assist them.

In a wholesale/retail transaction, your profit will generally be greater than in a straight wholesale/wholesale deal to a landlord or other investor. You can also call this strategy, *"Buy Low, Sell for More."* It will not be as great as a retail sale to an owner-occupant, which we will next explore, but that is okay since you will not have repair time or expense invested in the house.

What is the advantage for a sweat equity buyer to purchase from you?

As in any business, you get paid for your experience. You are also paid for your knowledge. You know how to find and buy property. Sweat equity buyers — either because they do not know or perhaps do not believe in investing in their own education — are choosing to do it all on their own. Therefore, you are the winner because these people are a valuable buying source for you.

You are getting paid because you have learned to maximize your profits. You know how to buy the house right, and know how to structure the sale.

Your investment in training and knowledge allows you to offer a valuable service and earn significant income.

In the final analysis, you are providing an extremely valuable service by culling out the bargains from all the available houses, then offering these deals to people whose plans, strategy, and priorities do not leave them time to locate them. You are providing a valuable brokering service. This service includes finding the deals and matching them up with individuals who are trying to fulfill their own investment strategies.

RETAILING THE HOUSE: "BUY LOW, SELL HIGH"

This strategy is similar to buy and hold, except that your exit plan presents itself much sooner. You select the wholesale houses you want to have repaired and you perform certain basic improvements which will make the house marketable. You then sell it to a retail buyer, perhaps an owner-occupant who wants to move in and have everything finished in the house.

These buyers will pay full retail for the privilege of having their houses in beautiful condition and ready to move into. After all, they are making the biggest single purchase of their life. They will evaluate comparable values in the area to see if they are getting a decent price so they will feel good about the deal they are getting. Their appraiser will confirm this to them. The bank will also confirm it. Why else would the bank approve the loan amount, unless the house was really worth it? These buyers are not buying a commodity; they are purchasing a home with all the emotional baggage this term carries. It goes without saying that a *home* demands more value than a house.

A word of caution: Do not lose focus.

Remember, your focus is in finding houses and making offers to purchase. Your pay as an investor will generally be greater if you have a contractor doing the repairs. Compute the costs of having a contractor do the anticipated repairs on the house to make sure your expenses are known before you make your offer.

Once this is done, calculate your expected profit on the house and figure how many hours the repairs would take you if you were to do them yourself. How much is that per hour? Remember, it almost always takes twice as long and costs twice as much when you do it yourself. The numbers speak for themselves.

Now you know how much it *really* costs for you to do the repairs yourself. You'll discover that your time is almost always better spent finding another deal.

With the mind-set of an investor, it becomes easy to understand that paying contractors to do the work often means more, not less, money in your pocket. When all is said and done, you will likely be happier having a construction professional handle detail items for you. This will allow you to keep your focus on the big picture, i.e. turning houses over on a timely basis.

Time Is Money

Finding and qualifying retail buyers generally takes more time, effort, and energy than simply wholesaling the house. Completing your first wholesale-retail deal from start to finish will spark an increased appreciation for this fairly simple way to quickly make a great deal of money.

Other Strategies for the Wholesale House: Buy and Hold Equals Money in the Bank

Buying and holding property is such a simple strategy that it is probably the most common one used by real estate investors on most skill levels. Instead of cashing out of a wholesale house, you will often choose to add it to your portfolio as part of your long-term investment strategy.

In essence, your "inventory" is your "bank." This is true because as you hold the houses and eventually pay off the mortgage (while they are increasing in value), you are building a bank account for your later years. You may be creating the funding for some specific future event, such as a college education for your children, emergencies, retirement, travel, and many other future needs. Because this is a long-term portfolio strategy, an entire chapter is dedicated to this concept in Section II.

Your tenants in these houses will often want to discuss buying the house from you, perhaps in the form of payments, until they can get qualified on a loan and can buy it outright. We will cover this situation further in the next section. We will include special methods that will allow you to lease a house with an option for the tenants to purchase.

9

MAKING FIVE MILLION DOLLARS A BELIEVABLE, ACHIEVABLE GOAL

———————◆———————

We have discussed (and will do so in even greater detail later) the subject of writing your business plan and setting goals for your business. Now it is time to discuss what is achievable today in the real estate investment business.

THE SIX-MILLION-DOLLAR MAN

Do you remember the television series about the man who was rebuilt using bionic parts? They used the phrase, "six million dollars" like it was a huge amount of money, and to some degree it was. Now we laugh in a movie when Dr. Evil threatens to hold the world hostage for a million dollars. He had been frozen for so long that he didn't have a clue about how insignificant that threat would be.

Although the rest of us have not been asleep in a deep-freeze, for many, earning six million dollars — or even one million — is our ultimate goal. In casual conversations, these are the figures used when talking about a great deal of money. Even so, is this amount really that much? Of course it is. But is it a large enough amount to be worthy of using it as a goal? Today I would have to say that it is not.

If you were to list your "wants," how quickly could you spend one million dollars? For some, this amount wouldn't even realistically pay for the house they want. Retiring on a million dollars is another scenario, but would it really be enough? If it lasted twenty years, it would amount to $50,000 a year plus interest. For some, that would be sufficient; but would it be the lifestyle *you* desire? What if you had a major expense or illness? How long would the money last then? I had a client whose health insurance was canceled on a technicality. His daughter's two unexpected surgeries cost $1,300,000. Tragically, this illness left my client penniless.

While misfortune and tragedy at one time or another arrives on each of our doorsteps, the manner in which we respond becomes an education in and of itself. It is essential to have the means to survive such a misfortune. Ideally, the "means" is much more than $1 million in available assets.

LEARNING TO TAKE EDUCATED RISKS

In the wealth-accumulating business, learning to take risks is a necessary mind-set to acquire. It must evolve independent of unforseen tragedy. Such a mental state is acquired one deal at a time. It must not be done willy-nilly, but in a controlled, calculated fashion.

Not long ago, my wife and I accompanied our daughter and son-in-law on a weekend jaunt to Las Vegas. We enjoyed ourselves immensely, especially the festive lights of the New Year's Eve celebration. We also enjoyed a spectacular evening of entertainment.

While we are not gamblers, during the course of the evening we were intrigued by the millions of dollars that were being "forfeited" by the patrons at the gaming tables. Many fortunes were likely lost during that one night alone. Adrenalin was pumping, liquor was being consumed, and money was changing hands with each roll of the dice. As spectators, we were more than a little intrigued to witness the lack of wisdom demonstrated by many of the visitors. It was as though they had arrived in Las Vegas with a predetermined amount "they would lose."

The wise risk-taker is not one who learns to play games of impending loss. He doesn't put a pre-determined amount of money into his checking account, then set out to lose it with a real estate purchase. Instead, it is his business to learn everything there is to know about a given property, then determine if purchasing it is worth risking his investment dollars. It is anything but a gambler's approach to accumulating wealth.

If taking educated risks creates fear in your heart, a loss of sleep, and total stress, then don't proceed. On the other hand, if "the chase" involved in finding a wise investment property makes you feel *alive* and *invigorated,* you are in the right business. Success breeds success, and success generally comes to a participant who gets a thrill out of the modest risk they are taking.

Through a lifetime of watching millionaire clients and incorporating their wealth-enhancing strategies in my own investment portfolio, I have made an amazing discovery. It is this: Investing in real estate actually allows a person to control his or her risk. This is true because they are involved in making the decision to buy a given property or to let it pass.

FIVE MILLION DOLLARS IS A DELIVERABLE GOAL

While one million dollars is a sizeable sum, a more realistic goal would be to have a net worth of at least five million dollars. This amount would put you into a range of comfort that is significantly more than the dollar difference would imply. Five million dollars meets all four criteria: it is a conceivable, believable, achievable, and measurable goal.

It is now time to learn the advanced secrets of my millionaire clients. Our goal is to explore exactly what it takes to accumulate a minimum of five million dollars net worth.

ACQUIRING THE MILLIONAIRE MIND-SET
—————————— ✦ ——————————
Twenty-one Advanced Strategies of
My Millionaire Clients

Now that you understand the basics of real estate investing covered in Section I, you are on your way to having a successful real estate investing business. To grow your real estate investing business exponentially, it is imperative that you begin developing advanced strategies early in your business evolution. How to move beyond the beginning investor to more advanced strategies is the focus of this section.

10

OPTIONS AND
LEASING WITH AN OPTION TO BUY

───────────── ✦ ─────────────

UNDERSTANDING THE SELLER'S MENTALITY

By definition, wholesale houses are in very poor condition. More often than not, their present owners have taken little pride of ownership in the property. It is a nuisance and has become a problem that they simply want to dispose of.

Attractive houses, on the other hand, usually have owners with completely different motivations. Their house is their home, their castle. They are generally aware of what their house is worth, although they may have been somewhat misled when they computed its value. They may have recently checked sales prices in the area, or an aggressive real estate agent looking for a listing may have given them an "educated" inflated price.

Regardless of the reason, sellers are usually not interested in deeply discounting their selling price. Because of this, different strategies must be used to make these deals profitable for you. Other investors have likely looked at the seller's house, then made offers to try and "steal" the property from the seller.

These sellers are generally savvy, they have money, and they know the value of their home.

Fortunately, I have observed several strategies that will allow you to take advantage of the scores of attractive houses available in your area. Understanding some of the seller's reasons for selling will help you understand their mind-set for selling their home.

TIME-INDUCED MOTIVATIONS

The seller's motivation is often not due to long-term financial problems, or to delayed maintenance of their property. Rather, it is from a deadline triggered by events. Their house is in good condition and is worth the asking price, but finding and getting a qualified buyer within their time frame is simply not feasible.

The following are time-induced motivations to sell a given property:

✓ Being transferred to another city (possibly against their desire)

✓ Building or buying a newer or bigger house (may or may not have a fixed deadline)

✓ The market is sluggish for houses in their price range or area (could be testing the waters)

The savvy real estate investor sees the seller's need to sell as their opportunity to purchase. Armed with your understanding and knowledge, you agree to offer the sellers all or most of what they are asking. They are shocked and wonder what the catch is. There *is* no catch except that you want to delay the purchase for up to thirty-six months. In the meantime, you will make their house payments and take care of all repairs.

Almost always, the seller's primary interest is to avoid dual house payments. You can solve their immediate worry by using the option approach and taking the time to maximize your own profit potential with the property.

How do you solve the seller's worry while making the deal profitable for you?

Leasing a house with the option to purchase at a future date may be the perfect investment strategy for you. Lease-options are not a strategy you would normally use on a wholesale house. However, it is perfect for buying an attractive house in a prime location.

In turn, you sublease the house you have just leased to someone who wants to eventually own it. You give them a second option to purchase the house within your allotted contract limits — and at a higher price than *your* option price. You may have seen deals like these advertised as "rent-to-own." Although these deals are a little more complex than a straight purchase and sale, you are entitled to three distinct sources of profit for your involvement:

1. When you sub-lease the property at the beginning of the contract, your lessee/buyers pay you an "option consideration" (this is similar to a down payment, but is non-refundable.)

2. During the contract they make monthly payments slightly greater than the current monthly loan payment (you keep the difference).

3. At the end of the contract, when you sell them the house, they pay you the difference between your "purchase" price from your seller and your "selling" price to the new lessee/buyer.

Why would the sellers not simply do this themselves and keep the extra money?

The sellers may be focusing on their new house, or on their move. Or, they may not know enough about leasing to feel secure. This can be true especially if they are moving out of town. In essence, you are offering them a management option, which will cover their house payment (often their main concern) and delay them having to deal with selling the house.

Of course, there are many questions that surface in this area, especially since you are dealing with a "retailable" house in an attractive area. When in this situation, we are often conditioned to think, "Something's not right," or "What's the catch?" Stated simply, there is no catch.

With lease-option and option deals, as with all purchases, we should remember our fundamental mission statement: We will only consider doing a deal if it is of a win/win nature between the buyer and the seller.

You can also use the lease-option strategy to move into a nicer home than what you currently own, and to do so at a price more in line with your budget. How is this possible? By covering the monthly payments, based on a mortgage made years earlier, you are making a payment that is often less than a new mortgage would be on the same house. In many cases, this means that you can live in the home for lower payments than if you purchased it outright, and still have the option to buy or sell at the end of your agreed-upon option term. Just as in the previous example, if the house increases in value between the time you sign the contract and the time you actually close the deal, you are entitled to the increase. It is your bonus.

How do you get a buyer qualified on the house if the seller has been unsuccessful in doing the same thing?

The answer is simple. You are trained and knowledgeable. You will lease the house to someone who would likely have difficulty in either getting a sufficient down payment or qualifying for the loan. Admittedly, this can include many people. This is an area where I personally relied greatly on my mentor to walk me through the various applicants, helping me select the ones to work with and the ones to avoid. I suggest you also confer with your advisor and take the time to study this area. Their experience can be extremely profitable, so it is worth your time and effort to approach it correctly and thoroughly.

THESE ARE *NOT* DEADBEATS

Good people often have "bad" things happen to them. These misfortunes can create a chain-reaction of events that damage their credit. These events may include divorce, a layoff, an injury, and many other unforseen financial "land mines." Tragically, these misfortunes wreak havoc with people who are honest and trustworthy. These persons are not deadbeats, drug dealers, or street people. They are good people who are simply trying to hang on. Often, a little "leg up" is all they need to get back in the saddle of self-sufficiency.

You can structure a workable option to purchase with affordable payments. This strategy gives the seller or buyer time to restore their credit and to get approved for a loan. In structuring a deal this way, you help the seller or buyer, while creating several different revenue sources for yourself. Everyone wins!

Millions of honest people who want a house, who need

a house, and who desperately dream of owning a house, cannot get one. Catering to those in need is indeed a niche market. Feed it and you will retire wealthy. Unfortunately, because of land mines along the road of life, many good people get treated like criminals. They cannot get approved for a loan through a bank or a traditional lender. When you creatively make it possible for these motivated buyers to own a home of their own, they will jump through whatever hoops necessary — and pay whatever price required — to make it happen.

Remember, you are not taking advantage of someone in this condition. To the contrary, you are literally becoming their lifeline to recovery.

Finding this need and filling it within your market area guarantees you a long line of motivated, quality buyers for your retail properties.

What if the owner simply does not want a tenant in his house?

This sometimes happens. A seller has a nice home and they want to keep it that way. If they are selling their home themselves (for sale by owner) and have not listed it with a real estate agent, you can ask for an option to buy the house. This agreement needs to be in place before they list the house, otherwise the agent's commission will generally need to be considered as part of the option price. If you sign an option with the seller, they can still list with an agent. The agent gets the commission, but only if he sells the house independent of your offer.

What is an option, and how does it work?

An option is more precisely an "option to purchase" a given property. Without going into technical legalities, an option sets an agreed-upon sales price for the house. As a buyer, this document gives you the right to purchase the house within a certain time period, perhaps six months to one year. During this time period, you can attempt to sell the house to a retail buyer. If you successfully negotiate a deal, you have the right to "close" at your original, agreed-upon price with the seller.

During the term of the option, the seller continues to make the monthly mortgage payments. While they do not get the debt relief offered in the lease-option strategy, they *can* continue trying to sell the house. If they (or their agent) gets a deal first, and you do not have a buyer, they can close the deal. For you, it is "nothing ventured, nothing gained."

How can it be legal for you to sell another person's house?

Generally speaking, without a real estate license you cannot sell someone else's house and earn what amounts to a commission. You can, however, sell your own house without having a license. The option agreement you signed with the seller gives you a legal "equitable" interest in the property. In other words, you have a contractual relationship involving that property. Ownership characteristics are now vested in you. This is a legal property interest enforceable by law as an equitable interest.

When a note is taken out to buy a property, and a mortgage is given to the bank, the property is "mortgaged." Even so, the buyer is still the owner. Legally, as we will see in the section on foreclosures, the mortgage and note give the lender an equitable interest that allows them, under certain circumstances, to take the house to pay the owners' debt, should the owner default. They are not the owner, but they have enforceable legal rights similar to ownership because they have an equitable interest in the property.

Likewise, with an option to purchase, though you do not own the house, the seller still does. Even so, you have an enforceable equitable interest in the property inasmuch as you have it under contract. In this case, the contract is an option to purchase. If you find a buyer and sell the property before the final date the option can be exercised, then you may buy it, sell it, and collect the difference.

What if I do not find a buyer and cannot exercise the option?

Stated simply, you walk away. The seller has nothing to lose and everything to gain by entering into an option agreement with you. The same goes for you. At the very most, you may lose a modest option consideration. Even so, this would likely be only a few dollars, not like the down payment/option consideration you would collect from a buyer. You have no further liability after the exercise date has passed, and neither does the seller.

IN CONCLUSION

Lease-options and options to purchase require more savvy than a simple wholesale/wholesale deal. You will want to take the time to study these concepts thoroughly and discuss them with your real estate advisor. The dollar difference you earn doing one of these deals, rather than doing simply a lower-priced wholesale/wholesale deal, can be significant. This difference can make these strategies some of the most lucrative deals of all. As you grow to understand them, you will expand your awareness beyond the lower dollar deals. You will move into an area where you can generate tens of thousands of dollars on a single transaction.

Just as in other areas we've discussed, having knowledge is the prerequisite to being able to take effective action. Utilize an advisor or mentor's knowledge and experience to guide you as you develop your skills in these exciting strategies.

11

THE WORLD OF FORECLOSURES

———————◆———————

LOAN DEFAULTS AND LEGAL RECOURSE FOR LENDERS

When someone is no longer able to pay their house payment, they are considered to have *defaulted* on the loan. The lender has an equitable interest in the property created by a legal document called a mortgage or trust deed and note. The owners previously signed these papers so the lender would loan them the money needed at closing.

In the case of a default, the mortgage or deed instruments give the lender the legal right to effectively *foreclose* on the property and demand that the owners pay the note in full. If the owners are unable to do this, they forfeit the collateral, which is the real estate itself.

Foreclosure is the process through which the courts and state law allow the real estate lenders to take control of and sell the debtors' ("owners") real property in order to pay the debt. Property in foreclosure is said to be *in distress.*

Distressed property goes through several stages of foreclosure. The first stage is known as "pre-foreclosure." Once the lending institution has begun the process of reclaiming the property, it enters what is called "foreclosure." When the property is auctioned to pay the debt, this begins another phase called "post-foreclosure."

You can buy the property at any phase of the foreclosure process — pre-foreclosure, at auction, or post-foreclosure. In each case, different strategies determine what constitutes a "good deal" for you.

Why do people allow themselves to go into foreclosure?

On the surface, it may be difficult to conceive of a person letting a house go and thereby losing any chance of getting a new mortgage loan for years. Still, this scenario takes place every day. People slip into foreclosure — sometimes passively, sometimes angrily, sometimes apathetically — but almost always in spite of everything they can do to avoid it. The following are several circumstances that frequently lead to foreclosure of a property:

Divorce This is likely the most common cause. Two people are often angry with each other, and uncooperative over their mutually shared assets and liabilities. Often neither is willing to bend, so both end up being financially destroyed. When a couple becomes antagonistic toward each other, nothing productive transpires, including the making of the house payment. Frequently the spouse who stays in the house cannot afford to make the payment alone; as time passes, the house goes into foreclosure.

Unemployment Layoffs, firings, downsizings, plant closings. Often, the higher the income and lifestyle, the more financially difficult this can become. Losing a job can lead one down the slippery slope to foreclosure.

Medical problems and failing health Encountering sudden medical difficulties, such as accidents or terminal conditions such as cancer or Alzheimer's disease can lead to default on the note.

Balloon payments on loans These are loans that come due after a certain date, perhaps after five or ten years. At the time the loan was taken out, the rate and terms seemed an eternity away. The arrival of a balloon due date can be the darkest day in one's life. When combined with any of the other circumstances, a balloon due date is a major trigger for foreclosure.

Death When the primary income producer suddenly passes away, the family's finances can vanish quickly. This is not as common as some of the other reasons, but it is a foreclosure cause that you will frequently encounter.

We have little control over the circumstances of life. We can, however, anticipate and plan, knowing we are not immune from misfortune. Even the scriptures say, "The rain falls on the just and the unjust." At the very best, the financial future for each of us is uncertain. The question is, will we individually take the investing steps necessary to prepare our own finances when bad times come?

By simply studying this book, you are miles ahead of the curve. You are obviously aware enough and motivated enough to take positive *proactive* steps to better secure your financial future.

Unfortunately, in the past many people who found themselves in foreclosure chose not to prepare for when times were kinder and gentler. As a result, they were not able to weather the storms of misfortune. Storms are often greater than all the preparation we can imagine. As we have discussed, people in foreclosure are not bad people. They are simply folks who have been hit with bad times.

In biblical times, all debt was forgiven every seven

years. In medieval days, the manner of resolving debt became much more harsh. These unfortunate people would have lost their house and been thrown in debtors' prison or sold into indentured servitude until their debts were paid. Foreclosure, in our day, is once again a helpful process. It closes the door on a person's debt. This relief allows them to eventually reestablish themselves and start a new life with more financial security.

It is important to remember that you did not create the problems a homeowner may be experiencing. Instead, you are offering a possible solution. Your solution may be their *only* viable way out.

FINDING FORECLOSURES IS EASIER THAN EVER BEFORE

There are many foreclosure-finding resources available today that were not available even a few years ago. Ask your advisor or mentor which ones they prefer to keep abreast of as properties move through the foreclosure process.

Not long ago, finding pre-foreclosures was largely a game of luck. If you knew a foreclosure attorney, they might have had advance knowledge of properties about to be foreclosed on. Foreclosure auctions gave public notice in the local paper, and getting through the bank managers in the post-foreclosure stage was iffy, at best. One of my clients made a fortune by becoming friends with an attorney who specialized in foreclosing on properties. Knowing the attorney who represented the banks and lending institutions made this client rich. On more than one occasion, he was the only bidder at the foreclosure auction.

Today, a number of services offer print and online

tracking of foreclosed properties through every phase, in every state, so you can easily find these exceptionally good deals. There is still research to be done on the individual properties, but finding foreclosures has never been easier.

Many public records showing liens and judgments on foreclosed property are now available online. Just as in other areas of real estate investing, (a) finding the properties, and (b) making suitable offers are the keys to your success in the foreclosure business. Is it worth including foreclosure properties in your business? Certainly . . . *IF* you remember this: **Your objective as an investor in foreclosure properties is to generate a twenty to fifty percent return on your investment.**

As an investor, these properties take more research, time, effort, and a willingness to get an understanding of the foreclosure marketplace. There are simple formulas to use in estimating values, repairs, and specific techniques you will use to negotiate discounted payoffs of other debts that may be attached to the property.

BUYING STRATEGIES: *PRE-FORECLOSURE*

Pre-foreclosure is the period when the owners still have the right to sell their property. The owners know they have a problem because they are in default on their note. They have been notified by their lending institution that their property is about to be foreclosed on, so it is no secret, except perhaps to their family, co-workers, and friends.

Depending on the emotional state of these people, they may be open to structuring a winning deal that will salvage a portion of their credit. They may be behind several payments (in addition to late fees), and at this point they get little or nothing from their lender. Obviously, if they have not been able make partial payments, they are likely not able to pay a lump sum of several payments.

This first phase of property foreclosure deals with people. The public makes a catastrophic mistake by thinking that real estate is only about buildings and land. This notion couldn't be farther from the truth. It concerns itself with people — the person or family presently owning the property. These people are in serious trouble, and so this period is a time when they are desperately seeking solutions to their problems.

People may experience financial hardship through death, excessive debt, sickness, job loss, job transfer, or divorce. Something unexpected hits them squarely between the eyes, and they stagger, dazed and unable to cope.

This state is something like a scene from the movie, *The Matrix*. In this movie, a bullet is fired out of a gun. The bullet flies in slow motion across the screen. The scene is very compelling and is visually impressive. It is while the financial bullet has been fired, or while a person is falling behind on their payments, that pre-foreclosure takes place.

Unfortunately, our society teaches us to prepare for gainful employment. We then go to school, or become trained, and are taught to be productive in a given profession. We are also often taught to work for someone else, rather than to work for ourselves. This mentality is frequently fatal.

Regardless of what hits us, when we then lose our job, we are ill prepared to continue making mortgage payments. We get behind and begin to experience a financial strangle-hold. This condition throws us into a fiscal and emotional tailspin, and we plummet into financial and emotional darkness. We are often still occupying our home, but every day we are unable to make our mortgage payment, we become more vulnerable to losing our position with the property. Because of this financial paralysis, we become more desperate.

It is essential to understand that the foreclosure process varies from state to state. There are judicial states and non-judicial states. There are mortgage states and trust deed states. The U.S. government operates under English Law, although there is one state that operates under Napoleonic Law. Still, the basic premise is that there are property foreclosure laws in all fifty states.

When initially purchasing a home or land, a loan is secured. The person or entity making the purchase becomes the mortgagor. The person or entity loaning the money is called the mortgagee. The loan on the property becomes a promise to repay, as evidenced by a promissory note obligating the mortgagor to pay the amount of the loan. The legal instrument giving substance to this note is the mortgage or trust deed attaching the loan to a piece of real estate. If the owner's (or mortgagor's) promise to repay the loan goes into default — and if the owner is unable to cure the note within a specified time period — they will lose the property. The bullet will hit, and the person's legal entitlement to the property will cease. If the property is occupied, the person or family occupying it will be evicted.

During a property's pre-foreclosure, as a potential buyer, you can actually visit with the owner and walk through the property with them. You are dealing with the owner/seller directly. Though you cannot give them what they may consider market value for similarly situated houses in their area, you may be able to pay off their loan balance. Depending on their equity, you may be able to pay them enough money to move, or to make a security deposit on an apartment.

One very wealthy client of mine uses this approach exclusively. He never goes to an auction. Instead, he visits and writes form letters to people in default. He has a very charming personality and genuine interest in saving his clients' reputation from an auction. He is truly perceived as a problem-solver for his people. Talk about win/win. This approach has made my client independently wealthy.

Another of my associates lived in New England. He worked for a firm that exclusively purchased homes in pre-foreclosure. He felt good about this since he was constantly helping families re-settle, often with some money in their pockets. In fact, he often found himself counseling them, giving them hope for the future. In his mind, this wealth-producing business was all about helping people.

If you are interested in researching properties in the "pre-foreclosure" condition, go to your county courthouse and ask to examine what is called the Mortgagee Index. This index will show when the mortgage was recorded. By computing the time lapsed from that date to the present (which may be a few months, or many years), you will be able to determine the approximate amount of equity in the property. Equity, of course, is the difference between the value of the property and any mortgage(s) on the property. Rather than mortgages, some states have recorded trust deeds.

The sellers have nothing to lose. To the contrary, they have everything to gain.

When a property goes into foreclosure, it will generally be auctioned for the loan balance plus legal and other fees.

Chances are, the owners will get nothing from the process. Because they are likely to get little or nothing if they choose to wait it out, you are not taking advantage of them by stepping in. In fact, you are probably giving them their last best hope at saving their credit and getting a small amount of much-needed cash from their equity.

BUYING STRATEGIES: *FORECLOSURES*

Once the foreclosure process begins, the lender turns the property over to an agent or a trustee — often an attorney — who in turn attempts to sell the property for enough to pay the loan balance and added costs. Usually this takes place at an auction or trustee sale.

Generally when a property is in foreclosure, an auction or trustee sale is held where investors are able to bid on the property. The first bidder will typically be the lender, who will bid the outstanding amount of the loan. This bid may also include legal expenses in processing the foreclosure.

If you are interested in purchasing a property that is in foreclosure, the first consideration should be to the person or family losing the property. This might include a phone call to them in an effort to help them through their difficulty. After introducing yourself, you may wish to walk them through the legal steps to foreclosure. Or, you may provide information on housing alternatives for them.

Working with people in this condition, without competing with other realtors and potential buyers, makes this investment strategy very appealing. It is also very rewarding as you are able to assist them in their time of dire need.

Once the foreclosure process has begun, legal and other fees are normally added to the owner's increasing debt. While the owner could still sell the property at this point, several factors combine to make this outcome less and less likely:

✓ The combination of loan balance, legal fees, and late fees may be too great for a new buyer to make the purchase

✓ As time passes, there is less time for a new buyer to get qualified on a loan (before the foreclosure process moves to the auction stage)

✓ Through misplaced resentment, anger, or despair the owners have allowed the property to slip into disrepair (or worse, purposely damaged it), making it less desirable

✓ The owners may have simply emotionally "dug in their heels," and are now resistant to doing *anything,* and may be automatically fighting anyone from outside their castle who suggests alternatives

LOCATING HOMES IN FORECLOSURE

When a person is unable to make their mortgage payments, the matter is turned over to legal counsel by the mortgage holder. When this happens, a *liz pendens* is filed against the property. This a Latin phrase that means "lien pending." It is a cloud on the property title. A date of sale will be determined at the county courthouse, and on that date the property will be sold to the highest bidder. From that date, the family has three or four weeks in which to vacate the premises. They are literally forced to leave, and if they do not voluntarily surrender the property, a sheriff may be forced to evict them, change the locks on the house, and restrain them from entering.

The information on properties in foreclosure is found in the courthouse of the county where the property is located. While some county computer facilities are sophisticated, many are not. In addition, many employees working in the real estate foreclosure division are not trained to be helpful in providing foreclosure information. Therefore, a potential buyer of foreclosed properties must be assertive.

When looking for a property in foreclosure to consider purchasing, my rule of thumb is to consider only those properties with a mortgage (or trust deed) that is at least five years old. Assuming a normal rate of inflation, this means that I will be examining properties with built-up equity. It almost goes without saying that equity plus motivation equals huge profits. If you are motivated, and if you take the time to examine elements of properties in foreclosure, you have the potential of making considerable profits.

RIGHT OF REDEMPTION

If a mortgagor or owner of a property loses their home, there are eight states that allow them to redeem their ownership in the home. Yes, even if the property has been lost in foreclosure and sold in a bank sale, the owner can reclaim the property by making up the amount of deficiency on the loan.

If you are living in a politically liberal state, you are likely in one of the eight states providing this "right of redemption." If so, and if you are interested in purchasing a property in foreclosure, you can request that the person in default waive his right to redeem the mortgage on the property. This can be done in a short letter that states:

"I hereby waive my right of redemption on said (give address and legal description) property."

Although a notarized signature is not necessarily required, I would strongly advise you to have the mortgagor's signature notarized with two witnesses. By taking these safety measures, you add an extra amount of legitimacy to the document.

AUCTION SALES

When attending an auction, or sale of property in foreclosure, you must have already lined up the cash needed to purchase the property. At the time of the auction — and if you win the bid by offering the highest purchase price on the given property — you must generally pay five to ten percent of the purchase price to the trustee holding the auction. In most states, the entire amount of the bid must be presented to the trustee in certified funds within twenty-four to forty-eight hours of the auction.

Most investors purchasing properties at auctions have a line of credit established at their bank, and they are able to provide certified funds within the allotted time period. When attending an auction, you may be the only person attending, or there may be other interested parties making bids along with yours.

If you have never been to an auction, I would highly recommend that you first attend one, without participating. Get a feel for the process and for expectations of when you do successfully bid on a property. For instance, if you bid prematurely, and are not able to have the entire cash purchase price by 4:00 p.m. that afternoon, or whenever the time deadline is, you are in serious trouble. You will not only forfeit the money you have given as a deposit on the property, but you will likely be banished from ever participating in a subsequent auction. This is not an area for novices or for those who are ill prepared to act responsibly.

As a word of caution, detach your emotions from the property you are bidding on. Many times I have attended auctions where bidders become emotional and even irrational. Some properties sell for more than their appraised value, simply because of the emotion-packed competitive spirit of the occasion. These events are highly energized, and can be exhilarating to attend — but you must remain detached enough to make sound financial decisions surrounding your own bid. Therefore, prior to attending the auction, determine a ceiling price you are willing to pay for a given property. Then, no matter how much pressure there is, walk away if and when the bidding price exceeds your assessed maximum purchase price.

To assist you in keeping track of properties in foreclosure, as well as future auction dates, etc., there is a computer software "foreclosure model" to assist you. This model manages your database so you don't miss an auction on a given property. This time line also allows you to help the person whose property is in default. It can assist you in being a problem solver for this person, as well as a property purchaser and manager for yourself.

Can you still save money at these sales?

Absolutely. A working knowledge of property values in your area is essential, something you will learn firsthand through experience with your coach or advisor. Properties are almost always sold for less than the retail market price. In addition, you will not be dealing with potentially emotional owners. Above all, pay close attention: Trustee Sales of properties are always sold "as is."

"As Is" Means *As Is!*

The property is sold just as it exists, with no quality or condition guarantees provided by the lender or owner. If the owner has damaged the property, or has allowed several years of disrepair to take place, *or* if the building has termites, if the roof leaks, or if the foundation has cracks, you will buy the property "as is." If the lender has set up a pre-auction tour of a certain property, by all means attend it. Take along a home inspector, roofing or plumbing contractor, or other experts. Their fee(s) will be worth it, I assure you. You may not have had the opportunity to inspect the property unless you did so during the pre-foreclosure stage. This is where your training and knowledge will give you the edge over investors who often bid "by the seat of their pants." Preparation, and paying for professional advise, are often the differences between a poor investment and one that is highly profitable.

One Client Strikes It Rich

Over a six-month period, one of my clients hired his unemployed nineteen-year-old nephew to do something both interesting and rewarding. His nephew attended every courthouse auction in his city during this time period. Doing so, he discovered two interesting facts: First, an average of only three to five other potential bidders showed up at each auction. Second, every property sold between fifteen and forty percent below retail value.

My client's nephew purchased fourteen homes during this six-month period. By the time he had resold these properties, my client made over $850,000 profit on this simple six-month auction-buying experiment.

My client further told me that they reached the point

where they did not even look at some of the properties they purchased. If they could buy a home from ten to thirty percent below the conservative estimate of value by the county assessor's office, they knew they had struck it rich.

On one occasion, I asked my client, "Did you lose money on any of your purchases?" He said, "No, our only letdown was making only $15,000 on one home. The other thirteen purchases were gold mines!"

AUCTIONS REQUIRE CASH

At a real estate auction, you will need to pre-qualify in order to participate. You do this by demonstrating that you can pay cash up to the amount you bid. This is often in the form of a cashiers' check. At some auctions, you must certify that you will deliver the funds within twenty-four to forty-eight hours.

There are "hard money" lenders in every part of the country. These are lenders who often require an equity interest in the property in return for supplying you with immediate cash. They will work with you so you can bid confidently, knowing you have the cash available.

You can also create a consortium of project investors, where you receive a cut in the deal for your knowledge of the business, or establish your own stable of hard money investors when you need cash quickly. We will explore both of these options in a later chapter. Yes, there is a cost to using other people's money (or OPM), just as there is a cost to using a bank's money. Having money on hand to make the deal is more important than the cost of the money itself. OPM is a powerful tool, especially when you have a good handle on your costs ahead of time. Your bidding will always reflect your anticipated expenses, leaving plenty of room for you (and your partners, or lenders) to profit. Finally, if you do not have enough room in the deal to "breathe financially" you simply do not buy!

Many auctions will allow you to post a deposit of between $500 and $5,000 at the close of bid. This deposit gives you a certain number of days to provide a cashiers' check for the remainder. You will learn ahead of time what the auction requires.

OTHER LIENS ON THE PROPERTY

Whenever a lender forecloses on a given property, not all liens are automatically extingiushed. You could still be liable for all or part of other liens and other judgments. Go to the county recorder's office and carefully research any property you plan to bid on. Be aware of the outstanding encumbrances to a clear title. You may be able to negotiate a reduced payoff simply by asking. If the combination of liens and judgments plus the purchase amount is greater than retail market value, pass up the opportunity to bid. In fact, my clients will generally pass on a deal *if* the combined costs exceed the assessed value of the property.

SO, HOW MUCH DO YOU BID?

The rule of thumb at an auction is to bid only enough to purchase the property, and never more than it is worth (taking into account outstanding liens and judgments). This formula seems simple enough, and if you are knowledgeable and alert, the bidding process will not create a problem for you. Unlike the retail market, most foreclosure buyers are unemotional about the process or the property. They will often start their bidding at sixty to seventy percent of the market value, and generally drop out if it exceeds eighty percent, thereby allowing less experienced bidders to buy the property. This is just business. They have their parameters and they stick to them. As a professional investor, so should you.

BUYING STRATEGIES: *POST-FORECLOSURES*

If, at a given auction, a specific property does not sell, the mortgage company who placed the minimum bid wins back the property by default. The question posed is: "What happens to the property now?"

In this instance, the property enters a category called real estate owned properties, or REOs. Banks sometimes call these properties non-performing assets, but from a technical perspective they are different. When a bank takes back the ownership of a property, this property does not automatically become an asset of that bank. It is a liability they must dispose of. Federal laws mandate that the property be immediately liquidated or sold.

Since this property is called a non-performing asset, rather than a bank liability, it must be sold as soon as possible. When banks are not able to liquidate their repossessed properties, the federal government can liquidate the assets for the bank. The government did this in the 1980s, when they formed what was called the resolution trust company, or RTC. Many lending establishments, particularly savings and loan institutions, were forced out of business at that time.

When considering a bank REO, we immediately know that this property must sell quickly. Banks usually sell these properties through realtors. These realtors become agents for the seller, which is now the bank. The realtor becomes a fiduciary, or a legally responsible agent of the bank. The reason this is pertinent at this point of the foreclosure process is that, when speaking with a realtor who is agent for the bank, you are giving the realtor information that can and *should* be given to the bank. This may mean the amount you are willing to pay for the property, the terms and conditions, etc.

When considering how much to pay the bank for a REO, consider what repairs the property will require in order to prepare it for resale. Consider the exterior, including the roof and landscaping, as well as the interior, especially the paint, carpets, and tile. Make sure you do not pay too much, just to own a specific property.

Although banks do not want to deal directly with potential buyers of their REOs, you can request an REO list. Sometimes, the management information systems, or MIS department, will have these lists. People in this department manage databases, including the REO database, and they will provide it to you upon request.

In speaking about REO's, and the opportunities available in this area, my associate James Smith says: "I live in a home in Florida that is approximately 5,500 square feet in size. I purchased it out of a foreclosure for $21.87 per square foot. And here's what's interesting. I couldn't have built it for that.

"Some people say, 'But, I want to build my dream home.' My reply is, 'Why build your dream home when you can purchase someone else's?' Luxury homes cost from $150 to $300 per square foot to be built and require a tremendous amount of energy and commitment. Many wealthy people experience financial setbacks and allow their homes to go into foreclosure. This is often the perfect way for someone to purchase their dream home, or even a dream home to re-sell on the market."

It is essential to remember that banks and lenders are in the money business. They are not generally in the real estate landlording business. They are burdened with a property they do not want, and they are definitely motivated to sell it. Above all, this motivation includes getting back as much of their money as possible.

By learning the motivations of the banks, and more specifically the REO officer at the bank, you will find that there is less competition for these deals than almost any other area of the business. One millionaire client of mine uses this REO strategy almost exclusively. His solid, cordial relationships with his bank's REO department has greatly enhanced his millionaire status.

REMEMBER: IF IT WERE ALL EASY, EVERYONE WOULD DO IT.

Foreclosure purchases are not in the mainstream of property acquisitions. On a general basis, you will not find them listed in the real estate section of your paper. When you do find them, it will usually be in the "Notices" section in the local financial newspaper, or in a specific online service featuring these distressed properties.

Like any legal processes, foreclosures can be a complex area for an untrained investor. Rather than seek competent training on the subject, many investors simply avoid them because of fear. If it were a simple process, everyone would be buying them. Because of this, often only a handful of investors show up at these incredible sales.

Your preparation and training will allow you to make a significant profit when the opportunity to acquire these distressed properties comes along. When it does, consult closely with your advisor so that you can readily take advantage of the best investment opportunities in your area. Remember, "good luck" is where preparedness and opportunity meet.

From my personal experience, few real estate investment opportunities provide greater quick returns than purchasing a property in legal foreclosure. Whether the intent is a short-term turn-around, a fixer-upper to rent, or a long-term property to occupy, this investment vehicle is remarkably lucrative.

IN CONCLUSION

The three phases of foreclosure are pre-foreclosure, auction or foreclosure, and post-foreclosure. Each of these phases maintain a unique position in your portfolio. One of the exciting aspects of this type of real estate investing is that it provides an entry level. There have always been foreclosures, and there always will be foreclosures. There will always be lower-end economy houses to purchase, as well as upper-end luxury houses.

When people experience financial difficulties, a wise, principle-based investor can provide timely assistance. Because most people who are in financial difficulties are emotionally and financially drained, they are often unable to think rationally to solve their problem. Your goal can be to attain financial independence, and hopefully you will remember to help others along the way.

12

TAX LIENS
CONTROL BY DEFAULT

◆

DEATH AND TAXES

A tax lien is one of the most misunderstood strategies of real estate investing. Even so, it can be an extremely lucrative vehicle for enhancing your wealth. This has to do with the unseen part of the real estate business: paper. Tax liens are not well understood by most real estate investors, but they should be in the tool kit of possibilities for every successful real estate investor.

Most real estate owners must pay taxes yearly simply for the privilege of owning real estate. Often this is in the form of yearly county taxes. Benjamin Franklin had it right when he said: "The only two things we can be sure of in life are death and taxes." Normally, most people pay their property taxes to their lending institution as part of their monthly mortgage payment.

Monthly house payments are a combination of four items. These are (1) Principal, (2) Interest, (3) Taxes, and (4) Insurance — "PITI."

The acronym "PITI" is usually pronounced by saying

each letter, not "pity," but P-I-T-I. Your principal and interest go directly to the lender, the principal portion to retire the actual amount you borrowed, and the interest portion for the privilege of using their money.

The property taxes and homeowners' insurance portion of each payment are usually put into a holding "escrow" account.

Escrow accounts usually have a small monthly fee added for the service of collecting and holding money. The owners do NOT receive any interest earnings on their money in escrow.

The escrow account may be handled by the lender itself, or by a third-party firm. Money placed "in escrow" is held until a payment is due. Escrow accounts do not accumulate interest on your money; in fact, a small monthly fee is usually charged for this service and is included in your monthly mortgage payment.

The lender uses the escrow account to hold the part of your payment that goes toward your homeowner's insurance and property taxes as required by the lender to protect their collateral — your house. Checks are then paid from the escrow account to the insurance company on an annual or semi-annual basis, and annually to the local tax collector.

When a house is paid-off, the owner becomes responsible for his or her own taxes and insurance payments. Since fewer and fewer people actively save money, this can become a problem.

Why is this true? Because even though the home-owners no longer have a monthly house payment, they are still liable for property taxes. Most property owners manage to keep their homeowner's insurance in force. Even so, when the tax bill comes due, they simply do not have the money with which to pay it. To make matters worse, property taxes generally increase from year to year, so every year the burden is greater. Let's face it, many people do not have the money management skills to plan for a property tax "hit" of several thousand dollars at one time. In some cases, they may still have a second mortgage payment or home improvement loan, but these loans do not usually include escrow taxes and insurance.

In addition, owners must still contend with the "stuff" of life. These include divorce, death, job loss, downsizing, and all the other variables that can knock the wind out of their financial sails.

When property taxes become due and cannot be paid, delinquency results. When this occurs, the county places a tax lien, or demand note, against the property. We may mentally come up with ways to cover our tax bill so this would *never* happen to us, but the fact is every year hundreds of thousands of people, institutions, and companies either cannot or *do not* come up with the money owed.

A sub-contractor can place a lien against your house if you do not pay them for the work they've done. This is called a mechanic's lien. It attaches like a magnet to the legal title of the property. It does not go away until it is paid.

When you are buying a house, you will often find one or more of these liens still attached to the property. They must be paid in full to clear the title. If properly motivated, the lien holder — in this case the county — can settle for a smaller payment. Or, it can sell the lien to someone else. The buyer of a lien is typically a sophisticated real estate investor. Amazingly, the county will often collect the tax money for you and pay it to you with accompanying substantial penalties and interest levied against the legal owner of the real estate.

Counties hold tax sales in order to get their money out of the liens and often let someone else try to collect it from the homeowner.

The normal practice in the United States is for counties to hold "tax lien sales." At these sales, investors can bid on an owner's unpaid property taxes. The procedure works a number of ways, but essentially investors bid on the amount of property taxes owed by the legal owner. Often the owner has allowed several years of back property taxes to go unpaid.

This is similar to a business that sells its collectibles, or accounts receivable or notes receivable, to a "factoring" agency. When this happens, it is paid cash on a percentage of what the customers owe. The agency is then allowed to keep whatever it can collect. In the case of tax liens, however, real property is the collateral, and in a sense you are the factoring agency.

If you are the winning bidder at a tax sale, you are obligated to pay the back taxes on the property. Generally with the county's help, you ultimately collect the money from the homeowner. The owner has a certain time period in which to repay you. If they do not do so, you are legally entitled to foreclose on their property. If they come up with the money with which to repay you, they keep their property.

Why would you do such a deal?

Not only do you get the money back that you advanced, but it comes with interest and often severe penalties imposed by state law. One of my millionaire clients works exclusively in tax liens. He averages a thirty-eight percent yearly return, simply by investing in tax liens.

You have control over their property by default: their nonpayment of taxes.

On any property title where money is owed, the lender in "first position" is usually the first mortgage holder. "Second position" might be the second mortgage holder. There can be a number of "positions," which simply represent the order in which the creditors are paid in the event of a sale. Of critical importance, tax liens generally become the first position, thereby replacing either mortgage or trust deed holders. This becomes a secure position for you as an investor in tax liens. In truth, it can be "manna (money) from heaven!"

ANY creditor who is owed money can foreclose on the property, demanding full payment of the amount due. In this case, this is the total of outstanding taxes and interest accrued and unpaid on a given property.

Any superior creditors — such as you as a tax lien holder, or a first mortgage holder, must be paid as part of the foreclosure process. Often the amounts owed secondary creditors are negotiable and even forfeited or reduced if the equity is not sufficient to pay them.

Also, as a tax lien investor there is no requirement that you auction the property, as in bank foreclosures (see the previous chapter on foreclosures). When the time period has expired, you can do whatever you want with the property. You may take occupancy, sell it, rent it, or even give it to a church or charity. You are literally the new owner without a formalized foreclosure procedure.

One of my millionaire clients acquired a Colorado Springs property worth over $260,000. He had invested only $14,600 in a tax lien certificate. The legal owner did not pay his property taxes within the statutory time period and lost the property to my client. This client recently told me, "Once or twice a year I am richly blessed because the legal owner does not pay his tax lien off and the property belongs to me."

In many cases, if the owners do not pay you the amount of the taxes, plus your interest and penalties, you can end up owning the entire property. When this happens, your return on investment can be 200 percent, 1000 percent, 2000 percent, or even higher.

There are many other unique techniques and strategies when buying and dealing with tax liens. With proper coaching and guidance, this millionaire strategy should definitely become part of your advanced arsenal of real estate investing.

Understandably, most investors do not appreciate how the U.S. tax system works. To clarify, we must begin on the local level. Every county has a tax assessor. Most tax assessors are politicians. Because they are elected, they may not be an expert in this field. This fact has been obvious in past Congressional hearings. One of our senators, or representatives, may be on a subcommittee without sufficient knowledge about the tax system. They are politicians and should be regarded as such. They mean well, but in the main they purchase software packages from vendors that automatically calculate property tax assessments for them.

Three Ways to Assess Property Value

There are three ways to calculate property taxes in the United States. The first way is by "comparables." That is, based on a comparable value of other properties in a given neighborhood, a tax amount is assessed on the subject property.

The second formula for determining tax value is called the net operating income, or NOI. If the property is a one-of-a-kind building, there are no comparables. This is true of the Nashville, Tennessee, Opryland Hotel. It is unique. To determine the value of this property, county assessors were forced to consider its net operating income. Its value was determined by the amount of net revenue generated on an annualized basis.

The final formula used to determine property value is to compute its replacement cost. Once again, this manner of assessing taxes is used when no comparative value can be determined. For example, the Mormon temple in Salt Lake City is a one-of-a-kind structure built over a forty-year period, from 1853 to 1893. It generates no income, but is used for religious purposes by the Latter-day Saint church. The only way to determine the taxable value of a building like this would be to compute the cost to replace it.

Since religious structures are not assessed taxes in the United States, we could perhaps consider another type of structure. This could be a building or stadium where professional basketball or baseball is played, but which could never generate enough income to pay for the building. Again, this method of determining tax value is used when the other two methods do not apply.

THE UNKNOWN ADVANTAGE

The thing most people in the United States don't know is that taxes supersede mortgages. That is, taxes must be paid before any and all mortgages are paid. Thus, if you are the delinquent property owner, you might ask: "Do you mean to tell me that if I make my mortgage payment every month, yet do not pay my property taxes, my tax certificate can be sold?" The answer, of course, is a resounding "Yes."

Therefore, what is the repayment remedy for the investor purchasing a tax certificate? Believe it or not, the investor can petition the court to allow the property to be sold for the back taxes. Taxes must be paid, pure and simple. If they are not, our schools close, our municipal buildings close, highway construction is halted; all government programs grind to a screeching halt. Thus, the courts provide preferential treatment to the tax payer — even when that person is an investor who purchased a tax certificate.

Each state has its own formula, with regard to the amount an investor can make by buying a tax certificate, and the amount of time lapsed before the courts can approve a sale for taxes.

James Smith adds: "I have an attorney friend who actually purchased a tax certificate at an auction for a piece of ocean-front property. He ended up with this property, which was worth many times the several thousand dollars he paid in back taxes. It was the ultimate water-front money maker."

All types of money-making opportunities have been found, purchasing property at cents on the dollar. It is not glamorous, but is an excellent way to build wealth. In a later chapter, we will discuss what you can do to have your retirement program purchase tax certificates. When this is done, all of the interest made will go into your retirement program, income tax deferred. It is a great strategy.

An Excellent Rate of Return

One of the appealing features of purchasing tax certificates is the unusually high rate of return on your money. On average, the annual rate of return is from sixteen to eighteen percent. In addition, in some states fees and late charges can be added to increase this return rate even more. The best approach to this type of investment is to investigate the rules and regulations of your state, and go from there.

As a concluding thought, it is important to know that purchasing tax certificates is legal in all states. No licensing is required to participate, no real estate license, or other credential such as insurance, broker/dealer, etc.

It has been my experience, and the experience of associates who routinely purchase tax certificates, that it is best to bid on certificates attached to properties you want to own. Don't burden yourself with a tax certificate on a property, such as a service station, where potential lawsuit exposure exists due to fuel storage tanks in the ground that may eventually leak. Keep your investment simple with single-family dwellings. This is a remarkable way to accumulate wealth, one purchase at a time.

In Conclusion

Purchasing a tax certificate is an excellent strategy to obtain a high investment return, a resort, a lake-front cottage, a second home, or an agricultural property. Purchasing tax certificates becomes the cornerstone for conservative investments. It is better and more reliable than some stocks, and even some mutual funds. It is an investment that allows you to take control of your own investments.

Assume, for a moment, that you purchase a property tax certificate and place it in your retirement program. This way, as we have observed, there is no current tax liability on the interest accrued.

From my experience, an aggressive approach to building wealth is purchasing a high yield tax certificate. It is aggressive, yet it is very conservative. In addition, the market is best during difficult economic times. There will always be tax certificate sales and opportunities to increase your wealth through this little-known vehicle.

13

THE BUY-AND-HOLD STRATEGY

———————— ✦ ————————

A SOLID ADDITION TO YOUR INVESTMENT STRATEGY

One of my millionaire clients worked for the U.S. government and was transferred every two years. He told me his secret: "Each time I was transferred to another city, I purchased the worst home in the nicest area of town, fixed it up, then moved two years later. By using this single strategy, I am now a multimillionaire."

As mentioned in Section I, buy-and-hold is an excellent strategy for long-term security. This strategy works as follows:

✓ You only select houses you want to keep for yourself

✓ You rent them out, letting your tenants pay the mortgage (along with some down payment and additional cash-flow in the process)

✓ Your expenses in each property are covered by your rental income

✓ You periodically choose additional properties to add to your investment portfolio

✓ Over time, your mortgages are paid down, and property values generally increase, so your net worth grows substantially

✓ Over time, your tenants' payments increase, creating an even greater cash-flow spread

When your property mortgages are completely paid off, you can use the ongoing cash-flow for additional income. You are also free to sell the property or to remortgage it. When this occurs, you free up tax-free cash with which to do more deals, thus repeating the cycle.

For many investors, buy-and-hold is their first and only real estate investing strategy. As in any investment plan, however, putting all your eggs in one basket may be an unwise strategy. A good mixture of the different strategies we discuss in this section should be part of your overall plan.

When you make a wholesale purchase, the buy-and-hold investors will become many of your top prospects for purchasing your property. When the right houses come along, the ones that meet your criteria, hold on to them as part of your long-term plan.

A REMARKABLE SUCCESS STORY

A millionaire New York client shared with me this simple but highly successful secret of buy-and-hold. It all started when he was a young, newly married college student. He used his $2,000 savings to make the down payment on a $21,000 duplex. He and his bride lived in one side and rented the other side for sufficient rent with which to pay most of their mortgage payment.

Four years later, this couple sold the duplex for $55,000. This allowed them to make $34,000 profit on their very first deal. They have repeated this process for thirty years. I asked him to share with me an example of a current transaction: "Almost five years ago, we purchased a two-bedroom condo in a nice location on the Upper West Side of Manhattan. The cost was $295,000. We rented it out for more than enough to pay the mortgage. Three months ago, we sold this condo for $765,000."

This couple made a remarkable $470,000 profit on the condo by simply buying and holding! For over thirty years they have practiced this simple technique. They now give credit to this investment approach for their $25,000,000 net worth.

Today, this couple is buying in the Harlem area of New York City, anticipating that the values in that unique location will increase in future years.

The amazing thing about this story is that this couple never made a concerted effort to buy real estate at wholesale prices. They simply paid full retail price on their properties, then sat on their investments for three to seven years. Today they are multi-millionaires, and all because they used this simple strategy.

LEARNING TO FORECAST YOUR PROPERTY'S FUTURE

As you develop confidence in a buy-and-hold investment approach, it is wise to consider the future value of your properties. You begin this process by carefully considering each of the factors affecting long-term economic and environmental growth. This is an ideal area in which to get professional assistance. A real estate investment mentor is well-equipped to teach you the various trends, pitfalls, and variables to consider. In reality, projecting long-term property value is easier to do than predicting short-term value.

While you are learning the buy-and-hold philosophy,

you would do well to consider factors crucial to the success of your investments. Although this is not an exhaustive list, it is a point of beginning that will help you into the "future value of real estate" mind-set:

1. Regional and local economic trends
2. Past and present real estate appreciation trends
3. City or county redevelopment trends
4. Area population trends
5. Area zoning ordinances, including future trends
6. Comparative property values

LOCATION TRENDS ARE IMPERATIVE TO KNOW

You have likely heard realtors proclaim the importance of "property location." Never is this more important than in buy-and-hold properties. What may be a suitable location today may become a death-knell to the marketability of your property in the future.

When considering location trends, it is good to step back and consider your *modus operandi* as an investor. Do you *invest* in a given property, or do you speculate by simply taking a gamble? Real estate investments are predictable, but they can be catastrophic if they are purchased without fully considering location.

One of my clients got off to a bad start with the purchase of his first two buy-and-sell houses. The first one was a residence, but was in a very poor part of town. He wanted to develop a buy-and-hold portfolio, so he fixed up the house and rented it out. The renters were late in making their monthly payments, then missed a payment completely. The tenant then did the unthinkable; he committed murder. He was captured and sent to prison, leaving his wife and children in the home with no means of support.

This family "nested" in the house rent-free for the next three months. Then, just as my sympathetic client thought he was going to begin receiving rents, the tenants moved without notice. Not only that, but they left the house stripped bare and in total disrepair. It took weeks and several thousand dollars in fix-up costs before the house was back on the rental market.

Discouraged, but not disenchanted, with additional savings my friend purchased a duplex. Again, the duplex was in an economically depressed area. Unbeknownst to my client, the renter sub-leased the house to a group of single men who were dealing in drugs. My client found out about the new "renters" when he went to the duplex to collect from the tenants he knew. Not only did it take three months to evict these new renters, but during the time they lived there they ruined the carpet, walls, and draperies by burning kerosene in the fireplace. They simply poured the kerosene over logs, and kept themselves warm through the winter.

Needless to say, it took my client and his wife two weeks to completely re-paint the unit. After replacing the carpets and draperies, they put the duplex back on the market. They had owned it for three years, and felt extremely fortunate to "escape" by getting their original money back. They never could get the smell out or recover their fix-up funds. What had promised to be a good buy-and-hold property ended up being a total nightmare.

Sadly, my client determined not to remain in the real estate investment business. Instead of rolling up his sleeves and more closely determining future value based upon the trends listed above opted to concentrate on the stock market where he suffered significant losses associated with declines in the market. He is now thinking about getting back into the real estate business. This time, however, he is using a mentor and is gaining a thorough understanding of the variables he should have considered in his first go-around. I have every reason to believe that he will do well.

IN CONCLUSION

When you incorporate the buy-and-sell strategy, you are wise to invest in good areas where the future appreciation of real estate seems assured. It is the same formula as having a quick turn-around property, only the analysis goes much deeper. Location is the most important consideration for buying any property, and the future location value will make all the difference in your level of success as an investor.

14

REOS – REAL ESTATE OWNED PROPERTIES

———————◆———————

As discussed in Chapter 11 on foreclosures, real estate owned (REO) properties are often sound investments. The purpose of this chapter is to consider them further.

After a property has gone into default and has been foreclosed on, this property slips into the misty recesses of the lending institution. It is filed behind a door with the initials REO, or "real estate owned." This department of the bank or lending institution usually has its own managers and staff. They are able to do almost anything they deem advisable in order to dispose of this property and the rest of their REO property inventory. They are motivated, but not always for obvious reasons. Their motivations often get mixed up, lost somewhere between "clearing the decks" and "holding the bottom line" for their department.

It is important to understand that banks shy away from property ownership, or REOs. Federal banking regulations restrict how much real estate the bank can own. This fact alone provides motivation for them to divest themselves of these properties.

Common sense would dictate that an REO property be discounted or repaired or handled in a way that might enhance its chance of selling. After all, at this point in the process, the bank has likely had the property in their liability inventory for at least a year. Instead, many banks allow their REOs to sit and deteriorate because lenders often want their money without doing any more work. They figure their work — their investment — was providing the loan in the first place, then going through the hassle and additional expense of foreclosing. An acquaintance of mine had his home foreclosed and the bank did not even winterize the home to protect it during the winter where temperatures often drop below zero.

Banks and lenders are in the *money* business, not the real estate management or investing business.

One obvious advantage of buying an REO property directly from a lender is that they alone have the ability to alter the "rules" of finance. For example, they may be willing to finance your purchase with little or no down payment, while including enough cash at closing for you to do the repairs necessary on the property. They can give you a moratorium on payments for a set number of months and thereby give you the chance to sell or rent the property. They often offer a deeply discounted price. The savvy investor will contact the lender after the trustee sale and make an offer to purchase. This begins the negotiation process. REO departments compile lists of their REO real estate and will often make it available to a potential buyer with a simple phone call.

One of my clients learned about the REO investment strategy while taking a university level real estate class.

Fortunately, his professor had experience with REOs.

Armed with the knowledge he had gained, this young student made his first REO deal. He simply called his own bank and asked if they had an REO department. To his surprise, he learned they did. He talked to the department manager who immediately sent my young friend a list of their REOs. My client looked the list over and decided to purchase a newly acquired REO from the bank. His choice was a thirteen-unit apartment complex that some "druggies" had been hanging out in.

My client paid $147,000 for the property. During the next several months he painted and cleaned, evicting several tenants. He even learned about being a landlord. By holding the property for several years, he sold it for $682,000. After expenses, he earned a nice $400,000+ profit on his first REO deal.

Know this: Until the REO property is sold, it is on the bank's books. It is an undesirable headache for them, and keeping it around is not a good thing for the lender. Nor does it look good for the REO manager.

REO managers are motivated to clear their inventory of distressed properties. However, as in any corporate environment, they also have senior managers to whom they report. They also have budgets and projections to meet, and bonuses to earn when they exceed projections. These variables affect their motivation to sell each property.

Sometimes asking several simple questions will reveal an REO manager's motivation for selling a particular property. Your questions may also identify another property you may be interested in purchasing from them. Cultivating this partnership, where you are viewed as someone who solves their problems while not creating new ones, is a major part of a successful strategy with these managers.

In Conclusion

Approach REOs with the same win/win attitude that you would have for any other offer, and you will find a willing partner in your real estate success.

REOs are not found exclusively within the banking system. The rarest REO investor I have seen is a client who deals exclusively with charitable REOs. I would be surprised if even one real estate investor out of 10,000 investors even knows about this rare but extremely profitable niche investment opportunity.

Unknown to but a few is the reality that churches and other charitable organizations often receive real estate as donations, or have other real estate they periodically wish to dispose of. One of my clients has one particular charity with which he does business. Every time the charity receives a real estate donation, they contact my client. He often buys this charity's real estate for discounts ranging from 15-40% of fair market value. He is happy and the charity is happy. The charity now has cash instead a non-liquid piece of real estate, and they are now more able to operate their charitable organization.

An administrator of this charity confided in me that this arrangement is nice for them because they do not have to manage the real estate and do not have to enter into listing agreements and go through retail sales negotiations. This is truly a win/win relationship for both. It is such a profitable strategy that this investor told the charity that he would purchase every piece of real estate donated to them.

I am convinced that someone reading this book will someday write and say: "I am a multimillionaire today because of this one idea alone." Without a doubt, it will happen.

15

THE SEARCHERS
CREATIVE "BIRD-DOGGING"

◆

MULTIPLY YOUR EFFORTS TO GENERATE MORE OFFERS

You cannot multiply hours in the day. On any given date, when midnight arrives, your clock starts over. You face a new twenty-four hours in a new day. As an investor, you can only drive so many miles, make so many calls, or meet with so many buyers and sellers. You are limited by the clock on the wall. By multiplying your efforts, you can generate substantially more growth and revenue in your business.

One successful method of accomplishing this is to create an army of people who are "sniffing out" possible deals during their day as well. They may be doing this passively by recommending you when someone mentions they want to sell their house. Or, they may do it actively, as a part-time effort to boost their income, or even full-time if they become an expert in this field.

This network of bird-dogs are searching for undervalued properties — deals you can't pass up. They are invaluable in assisting you as you amass your wealth. They may include family, friends, mortgage company employees, accountants, attorneys, property managers, real estate agents, and landscapers. They are individuals who are "in the area," observing properties and their value.

If you are just getting acquainted with the area or market, give a calling card to everyone you meet. Let them know of your need, and how you can assist them in earning a second income. Let them know that you simply need a property address, a disgruntled owner, or a property that is distressed and for sale at a discounted price. You will be amazed by how many people will come forward when there is a fee involved. When retaining someone's services, state explicitly that a fee will be due and payable *if* and *when* you close (or purchase) a property they locate for you.

DO WHAT YOU DO BEST

As you are considering your real estate activities, come to grips with what you do best. Knowing you must oversee the complete property acquisition and selling process, determine the portion of it that brings you the greatest satisfaction. Once you have done this, learn to delegate. Some people call this process the "leveraging of people." Other participants allow you to lengthen your stride and multiply your footsteps. In a very real way, they are a vital key to your success in this business. There is an old adage that goes like this:

> That which we persist in doing
> Becomes easier to do;
> Not that the nature of the thing has changed,
> But that our ability to *do* has increased.

Once you have found the part of this business you enjoy doing best, repeat the activity again and again.

Become an expert in this area, and you will maximize your investment potential.

The way to find people who are able to assist you is to look for them at the same time you are looking for good properties. Instead of blindly looking for properties themselves, consider those persons you meet along the way.

BIRD-DOGGING DEFINED

The term "bird-dogging" refers to paying a finder's fee to someone for bringing you prospective houses and buyers, or for the actual deals that result from their efforts. Just as individual sellers have different motivations, some of your bird-dogs will want to work for part of the deal. Others will be more comfortable with the "piecework" approach where they earn money for each lead they bring to you.

Obviously, the bird-dogs who are paid per lead will earn much less per house than the ones who hold out for part of the deal. Your confidence in your own abilities, and the integrity of your bird-dog, will ensure success using this technique. One single deal can pay for hundreds of leads.

VERY NORMAL RETURNS

One of my clients made over $8,000,000 profit by using a bird-dog on only three deals. This was his strategy. He contacted a real estate broker who was a nice guy, but who was struggling financially. He offered the man a special bird-dogging commission of three percent on top of normal real estate commissions if he were to find a property suitable to purchase. In addition, the broker would earn a $10,000 cash bonus for finding three separate properties on which my client could build a commercial complex he desired to build.

The agent likely devoted ten hours per week to this search. It took three months to find the first location. My client was thrilled because it satisfied the parameters for his type of building. The second location was secured a few months later and the third soon thereafter. All three real estate properties were acquired in less than eighteen months. The bird-dogging agent was ecstatic. It was his best payday ever! My client was even more elated by making over $8,000,000 profit on the three commercial buildings he built on the three sites.

I have another client who gives a small, one percent bonus at closing to another bird-dogger. This client specializes in buying homes of approximately 1,000 square feet in a western state where such homes are considered on the small side but in high rental demand. This client's bird-dogger is thrilled to get regular bonuses this way and has found dozens of properties for my client. When they began working together, my client gave his bird-dogger specific parameters to look for. In fact, my client showed me the one-page checklist on each potential property the bird-dogger finds.

More leads, more offers, more deals, more money. Bird-doggers who want a piece of the action can also be a good source of leads. You can require and receive more complete information from these sources, since in a way they are partnering with you. They may even learn to ask the seller certain pre-qualifying questions before bringing you the lead. This approach allows them to filter out unmotivated sellers. They have the incentive to bring you good prospects, not just a list of houses.

You may pay a flat amount of several hundred dollars for a closed deal. Or, you may pay a percentage (often five percent) of the anticipated profit. Either way, you will get a high-quality lead and a foot soldier who will do what it takes to find sound investments for you.

IN CONCLUSION

In analyzing the value of bird-doggers, consider the value of your time. If they can bring you five or ten extra leads each week, that is 250 to 500 new prospective houses you can make offers on each year. You may quickly find that your bird-doggers are your best source of qualified leads. This one strategy alone can keep your waiting list full and give you more time to simply make offers and close deals.

Remember this: Your ability to make offers and close deals means that bird-dogging fees are a remarkable bargain.

16

MOBILE HOMES

———————————◆———————————

Imagine a house that depreciates like an automobile, yet which generates consistent revenues.

Investing in the niche market of mobile homes is an unheralded gold mind. Although it is anything but glamorous, it can catapult your wealth.

When considering an investment purchase of a mobile home, above all do not buy such a dwelling new. Let someone else take the depreciation. Purchase it when you find it at a bargain price, and allow it to add cash flow to your portfolio.

Several years ago, mobile homes were called "trailer homes." Within the industry, they are now referred to as "manufactured homes." Whatever you call them, they can mean remarkable revenue for you.

BUYING WHOLESALE TAKES ON A WHOLE NEW LIGHT

Unlike a wholesale house, a used mobile home may not need many repairs. It may be a repossessed unit or one where the owners have gone into bankruptcy. They may have been transferred or they may have obtained a divorce. In this sense these deals are similar to foreclosures, but without the courts and auction process to contend with.

Would it surprise you to learn that people purchase beautiful mobile homes for $30,000 to $75,000 and more? This does not include the cost of the land, which is generally rented or leased. Five years later, the owner is fortunate if the mobile home is worth half of its purchase price, and the mortgage balance may be greater than market value. When a unit like this is repossessed, you have the option to purchase it from a financial institution or dealer for what often amounts to a ridiculously low price. As a rental, these homes can often provide $750 or more cash flow per month, thereby creating a significant source of revenue for you as an investor.

One of my investor friends purchases mobile homes, then resells them and "holds" the mortgages. He then sells off the first few years of the mortgage, usually for enough money to cover his cost of purchasing the home. He gets his money out, his investor gets payments for five years instead of him, and he has the means to do another deal.

After five years of doing this, my friend began to receive dozens of monthly payments, with zero costs involved! We will cover more about this under the section on "paper."

IN CONCLUSION

You may dislike mobile homes, or you may think they are tacky, cheap, ugly, and wobbly. These sentiments are understandable, yet not relevant to the investor mind-set. You do not need to live in a mobile home in order to make money from purchasing them. Every mobile home needs two things to be livable — land (or a pad) and utilities. You can provide the land, electricity, water, and sewer. You can either rent out the spaces or buy inexpensive mobile homes, then either rent or sell them to eager occupants. You can generate the rental of three to five mobile homes for the investment you would normally have in one or two fixed dwellings.

17

VACATION HOMES

◆

EVERYONE WANTS TO "GET AWAY"

It has been my observation that people are spending more and more discretionary money on entertainment and vacations. While it may not be practical to own a year-round beachfront condo or a house at the ski slopes, why not consider such a house for the dual purpose of an investment piece of real estate as well as a vacation retreat?

One of my millionaire clients, who loves to both travel and make real estate investments, uses this approach almost exclusively. When I last talked with him, he owned vacation homes in New York City, San Diego, Park City, Las Vegas, and other locations. In all, he and his wife have ten vacation homes. But even though his family visits and enjoys each of them, they are houses, not homes. These ten dwellings are commodities, investments for my client.

This client tells me that if he needed the money, he could sell any of the ten at the drop of a hat. Over the years he has seen an approximate fourteen percent annual return on these investments. One vacation home netted a low six percent annual return, while another averaged a thirty-eight percent annual appreciation rate of return. In my last consultation with this client, he informed me that he is considering trading one of the ten for a chalet in the Swiss Alps.

A MARVELOUS REALITY

Does owning a vacation home sound like a dream? It is absolutely real. If you are going to buy real estate, why not have some fun with it? If you like skiing, making trips to your favorite slopes several times a year can really add up. Why not buy a place and plan your trips to check out your investments? In addition, your travel may be deductible under Section 162 or 212 of the Internal Revenue Code. When not visiting, you can often collect the choicest rental rates available, with high-quality individuals who do not mind paying top dollar to stay and play.

Buy your properties according to your interests. If you like going to the beach, buy on the beach. If you like trips to Florida, buy destination areas in Florida. There are thousands of golf courses around the country and many resorts in almost all states.

What do you think happens when a house adjoining a golf course needs to be sold? It is a high-end niche market, and as such may not sell as readily as a more "normal" house would. This is because not everyone wants a house on a golf course or on the ocean. High-end houses often take longer to sell because the income levels required to purchase them are higher. After reading the previous chapters, you should know that both of these "problems" create the best scenario possible: motivated sellers!

WHAT IF VACATION HOMES ARE OUT OF YOUR PRICE RANGE?

A lease with an option to purchase can be an excellent strategy to use when acquiring vacation properties. Collect the cash-flow for several years, then sell and acquire others. A little later we will be discussing using other people's money as well as creating a consortium. The short answer is, there are many ways you can purchase vacation properties. The advantages can be staggering.

UNDERSTANDING SEASONAL FACTORS

Vacation destinations have their hot or "peak" season. The rest of the year they do not have as much demand. This means you may be able to generate several times normal rent during the season, then rent it out for a nice cash-flow during the "off-peak" times of the year. Month-to-month and even week-to-week rentals are not uncommon in these areas. Even so, if a tenant wanted to make a longer commitment, you have the option of locking in a long-term lease or selling the property outright.

If you wish to personally use the property for a portion of the year, you should opt for the off-peak times. This is a common-sense mind-set for an investor. Of course, if you want to ski your favorite slopes and stay in your vacation home, you have the choice of doing so. You can still collect weekly or monthly rentals the rest of the year to cover your expenses. The client I mentioned earlier with the ten vacation homes has an interesting philosophy. He typically uses the Park City, Utah, house in the summer during the lower rent season. He then makes it available for lease during the highly-profitable winter/snow season. He has a winning formula and is able to enjoy his investments along the way.

IN CONCLUSION

Investing in one or more vacation houses is different than buying a vacation *home*. If your family desires a special vacation home that is convenient to where they all live, then by all means buy a property that can help build family traditions and memories. Our discussion is not about these homes. Vacation houses are expendable, financial considerations.

As we mentioned in an earlier discussion, remaining detached from a particular dwelling is essential to making sound financial decisions about buying and selling your properties. This is never more true than it is with vacation houses. Even though "maximizing eventual earnings" is the essential investor mind-set, that does not mean you can't utilize and enjoy your real estate investments along the way.

From my experience, the most astute millionaires have this mentality. Almost every property they own is for sale. After all, where one vacation property is for sale, an even better one is available to purchase. After all, a change is as good as a rest. Many of my wealthy clients enjoy rotating their vacation properties just *for* the change. For them, variety really is the spice of their investment life. Even more specifically, owning a variety of vacation houses is the frosting on their investment cake!

18

APARTMENTS

———————◆———————

THE MARKET ADVANTAGE

From an investor's viewpoint, owning one or more apartment complexes is a unique strategy. In terms of complexity, they fall between single-family dwellings and commercial real estate. Admittedly, any rental can be considered an apartment, especially when it includes a duplex, four-plex, or a similar multi-tenant dwelling.

As an investor, you must put on the "landlord hat" with any of these apartment types. Even so, the dynamics of your job description automatically change as the number of your apartment units increases.

When buying an apartment building, incorporate a "commercial property" mentality.

As you are determining whether or not to purchase an apartment complex, you must consider the value of the units in terms of their cash flow. Just as with office buildings, strip shopping centers, storage units, and other types of commercial real estate, the value of the property on the land is not as important as the value of the rental income harvested each month. Figuring your ROI, or return on investment, is an important part of your decision-making process. Determining your net monthly cash flow, making sure you are covering your costs, is another.

A simple rule of thumb is to make sure you are always able to cover your basic costs, including taxes and maintenance. Your computation should be made based upon only a fifty to eighty percent occupancy of your rental units. This allows you some financial "wiggle room" so you can do routine repairs, make improvements as needed, and conduct scheduled maintenance such as repainting or recarpeting. It also allows you to pay for cleanup after a tenant moves out, as well as provides you with time to qualify and rent to a new tenant.

As another rule of thumb, plan on budgeting a percentage of your revenue for managing and maintaining your apartments. Keep close to the project and try to anticipate its maintenance needs. As in life, there is no maintenance crystal ball. As with automobiles, however, scheduled maintenance on the project gives you the edge.

EFFECTIVE WAYS TO ANALYZE PROPERTIES

When considering a given property, insist on the seller providing you with the property's historical profit and loss statements, focusing on its internal rate of return, or IRR. This amount is the return after taxes are paid.

There are two types of returns to examine. These are (1) the growth rate, and (2) replacement costs. These are discussed as follows:

Growth Rate: These projections are based on historical trends. By utilizing an analysis of this rate, you will obtain a very conservative IRR.

Replacement Costs: Future replacement costs related to the project provides an aggressive IRR. It is based upon projecting a future selling price based upon these costs. It will give you solid data in terms of the profit you can expect when you sell the project.

As a caution, remember that when you are in a down market, your goal is to purchase a given property as far below current replacement cost as possible. To determine this cost, ask local building associations to loan you a copy of the *Marshall & Swift Valuation Service*, or M&SVS. This booklet provides information on construction costs of various types of apartment complexes in different regions of the country. Learning to use this tool can be greatly enhanced in consultation with your selected real estate professional.

Remember, when you move into the investment strata of apartment buildings, you have become a sophisticated investor. This certainly doesn't mean that you know everything. What it *does* mean is that you know where you must go to (a) learn what you need to know, and (b) make a decision about purchasing a given property.

There are five ways available to analyze a given property. Although the purpose of this book is not to give details in analyzing investment opportunities, at least knowing about them is essential. They are:

1. Comparable sales data, or "Comps"
2. Qualified appraisers, with appropriate credentials
3. The "gross multiplier" method
4. The "capitalization rate" method
5. A uniquely sculpted computer program

As you can see by simply reading through these appraisal methods, understanding apartment complex values is a very sophisticated process to learn. Still, it can be done, and you will gradually gain a comfort in this arena.

MARKET TIMING AND PROPERTY LOCATION

As you consider whether or not to acquire a specific apartment complex, take time to examine market conditions. Learn the idiosyncracies of the local area, and understand zoning restrictions, rental ordinances, etc. Several years ago one of my clients purchased a nice 126-unit apartment complex in Houston, Texas. He and his partners did everything correctly, netting a nice $800,000 profit when they sold the project nine months later.

Enthused, my client looked the entire area over, locating a 156-unit apartment complex several miles southwest of the first, in the shrimp harvesting city of Baytown. Investing the money they had just made in a tax-free exchange, they soon owned this larger project. What they could never have anticipated, however, was that three or four months after taking ownership in the project, the shrimping business died. Prices fell, the economy collapsed, and the area became almost a ghost town.

My client and his associates kept the complex 100 percent occupied, but only by nearly giving away the units. They were forced to offer several months rent-free, as well as other enticements, until they found themselves being forced into a quick sale. By the time they sold the property, they had lost all of the profits they had made on the first complex, plus an additional several hundred thousand dollars. The lesson they learned is this: Never own an apartment complex where the local economy is primarily reliant upon a single industry or employer. The risk is simply too great.

Snake-bitten, this same investment group constructed a 65-unit apartment complex in a perfect rental area of Salt Lake City, Utah. By the time the complex was completed, however, the local Utah economy collapsed. It was during the mid-1980s, when interest rates soared to twenty-one percent. My client and his partners were again forced to sell. Even with 100 percent occupancy, the global economy was not able to support the apartment unit growth factor.

To summarize, caution is the better of valor when considering whether or not to buy an apartment complex. Even so, there are times when factors beyond our control impact the viability of a project. Be cautious, do your homework, and success will almost always follow.

GETTING A GOOD BUY IS POSSIBLE

Just because an apartment complex is a bargain does not mean the property is a problem. Again, as with automobiles, "used" ones do not guarantee problems. Most people care for their cars, eventually trading them in or selling them to another owner. When considering availability of an apartment building, realize that some life change or business change has made the units available. Apartment complexes are bought and sold everyday, either because of poor management, because of an upgrade to a larger complex, or because of a change in objectives.

BECOMING A NEW OWNER

When you become a new owner of an apartment building, you often have the opportunity to renegotiate existing leases. If you are able to do this in your area, by all means do; that is, if the market can bear an increase.

In addition to cash flow considerations, if there are problem tenants the previous owners were bound to, now is the time to break the tie that binds. Some new apartment owners take the extreme option of giving all of the existing tenants notice, then having them each re-apply and re-qualify. Unless you have significant repairs or feel you need to "clean house" by replacing some of your tenants with new renters, this is a drastic step. More often, a new landlord will announce new lease increases, or an adjustment in fees.

Above all, as a new owner establish your rules immediately. Even if you do not increase the rent, common sense should be the rule. For example, if you have a person residing in one of your apartments, you should have their name on a signed lease, and their credit report in your file. Before your tenant sublets or sub-leases to another party, (which is the acquisition of new roommates), make sure you are given the right to accept or reject them. Your authorization, or that of your manager, makes sense. It is the only way to run your apartment portfolio business.

The sale of their apartment building or complex can often lead to uncertainty and rumor among the tenants. After the closing, send a letter to each tenant. Depending on the circumstances, you may even want to have a general meeting with them. Remember, as a professional landlord, you must maintain distance between yourself (or your manager) and your tenants. You are not their personal friend, their buddy, or their counselor. You are their landlord. Make it clear that you are open to hearing their needs and concerns, but that they must abide by your rules so that the apartments, as a whole, will be the best possible home for all the residents.

Rewarding "Good" Tenants

Just as important as establishing your rules and guidelines is letting it be known that you reward good tenants. Special renewal bonuses, extended lease options, gifts, and personal recognition provide incentive to live by your rules. All of these incentives go hand-in-glove with clear and concise rules and guidelines.

Delegate or Stagnate

When owning or managing a group of apartments, the key elements to success include (1) the rentals themselves, (2) monthly collections, and (3) property and building maintenance.

Some successful landlords choose to start their own management company to handle each of these areas. It has been my experience that if you are dealing with a hundred or more units, this strategy makes sense. Otherwise, plan on building into your budget the costs of having a management service handle the rentals and collections — all interaction with tenants. As a second part to this strategy, retain the services of a maintenance group to take care of the property repairs. This may be the same management company that deals with the tenant, or it may be totally independent. Usually the availability of such service companies will determine your approach.

When considering how to manage your project, you may wish to review the chapter in this book on Property Management and Landlording. Unless you are interested in structuring a management/maintenance company as a profit center for your business, the smaller number of apartments you are working with, the less realistic it is to handle all of this by yourself. It is better to be out finding your next deal. Remember, time is money, and as a serious investor you can't afford to be "dime wise and dollar dumb." Your first and foremost priority is to make money, and you do this by acquiring and selling properties as frequently as circumstances allow.

Long-term Cash Flow

Just as with other commercial properties, well-purchased and well-managed apartments can be a marvelous ongoing stream of income within your portfolio. As with all rentals, your apartment tenants will build your equity until ultimately you own a free-and-clear cash cow!

Knowing When to Sell

Just as essential to understanding the buying process as it relates to larger properties is the need to know when to sell them. When ascertaining the optimal time to do this, you must consider 1) economic trends, 2) market conditions for your particular type of apartment complex, 3) the "saleability" of your property, 4) cash flow losses or gains, as well as, 5) the tax ramifications for doing so. Have major changes occurred in the vacancy and rental rates of your units? Have the replacement costs per unit matched the selling price per unit you can expect to realize?

Above all, when considering whether or not to sell, obtain legal as well as industry counsel. In selecting a broker to market your property, choose the most seasoned apartment selling professional in your area. This is no time for sentimentality, for selecting a neighbor, or for selecting someone from the Yellow Pages. Choose wisely, and you will forever be glad you did.

As a caution, before selecting a broker to market your property, obtain an MAI appraisal. It is a small price to pay, but essential if you expect to attract a credible buyer.

IN CONCLUSION

When you are considering purchasing an apartment, ask the seller to provide you with a folder complete with notes on existing tenants, including their credit and payment record. Review this report carefully, for it will reflect the viability of your client base. Also examine information on upkeep and repairs, condition of carpets, draperies, roofs, landscaping, and utility requirements, etc. Find out everything relating to the condition and cash flow requirements of the project. Only then will you be able to make an informed decision regarding the viability of the complex.

After reviewing all numbers and renter information make your final decision based on dollars and cents. All other things being equal, if the ROI is good — and if the location and local economy is right — buy!

When it is time to sell your property, or to determine if it is the optimal time to sell, be just as thorough in your investigation. After getting an MAI appraisal, select the consummate professional listing agent to assist you. Simultaneously, retain the services of a real estate attorney. He will be able to determine tax consequences, contract suitability, etc. Selling a project, and the method of doing so, is as important to do correctly as buying the project is. It is a team experience on both ends of the deal and can accelerate your financial growth in staggering proportions.

19

EXOTICS

———— ◆ ————

If you think owning vacation houses is an exciting niche, what about owning a castle in Europe?

Exotic houses are unique, absolutely beautiful properties that are in an investment world of their own. They attract a special buyer, one who desires to own more than a mere residence. The buyer wants a showplace and will pay for the privilege of having one.

Imagine a luxurious house jutting out the side of a mountain, surrounded with limitless views and rugged landscapes. Or, conceive in your mind a house on an island, including the entire island as the real estate attached to the house. It is almost a *Ripley's Believe It or Not* statistic, but worldwide there are almost 3,000 islands that qualify for their own sovereign nation status!

Is this too much of a paradigm shift for you? What about a fifteenth century castle in Europe? There are literally thousands of these still in existence, and they often become burdensome for their owners. For less than the price of a home on the eighteenth hole of many United States golf courses, you could own your very own castle. Once the deed is signed over to you, you are almost automatically "landed gentry." This is a conferred title that is often transferred with the property's deed.

EASY ACCESS THROUGH THE WORLD WIDE WEB

Do you now see what is meant by "exotics?" With the advent of the World Wide Web, these properties are easier than ever before to find, negotiate on, and purchase. Likewise, they are easier and easier to sell for a profit.

While writing this chapter, I decided to have a five-minute exercise on my home computer. I logged on to the Internet, then typed in the words: *Exotic Luxury Houses for Sale.* Immediately a web site appeared with fifteen sites on the first page alone. These included luxury houses, land locations, hotels, and condominium homes and apartments. A most intriguing site was for "six Riviera sun villas for sale or rent." Try it; you may find the Riviera property of your dreams, one that will net you the highest return to date . . . that is, if you can bring yourself to sell it once you have vacationed there!

TAX-FREE PROPERTY EXCHANGES

While wise investments are always sold at a profit, one of the ways this can happen in the "exotics" market is through tax-free exchanges. If you pursue it, you will find organizations that specialize in helping investors exchange their properties for newer (at least to the investor) and more exotics. In fact, over 50,000 professionals and private investors belong to 150 local real estate exchange groups. Most of them operate as nonprofit associations and can be very stimulating to associate with. Whether or not you own a tropical Pacific island and you want to exchange it for a castle in Europe, the opportunities are almost endless.

When planning for maximum success in exchanges, it is essential that you be properly educated. Once you learn how to invest in this manner, it is mandatory that you maintain impeccable standards. To establish your reputation, the need for professional integrity cannot be overstated. You will soon develop a reputation that will hopefully make you a desirable exchange partner, one that other investors will want to "go to escrow" with.

LAYING TO REST LONG-DISTANCE CONCERNS

Some investors are not inclined to purchase exotic properties that aren't located in the area in which they live. For them, traveling to Europe, to the Carribean, or to the Pacific has no charm. Be that as it may, if you are the adventuresome type and enjoy traveling as a tax deduction, such an investment can be profitable *and* exciting. No matter where you buy properties, you will eventually reach a level where you hire management firms to oversee, rent out, and eventually market your properties.

One of my Texas physician/clients has this "exotics" mind-set. He also has a love for European history, culture, and people. For years he and his family have vacationed in France and England, often at exotic castles. Today he and three friends are pooling their excess resources and purchasing an English castle. When I learned of their plans I was shocked at how little this "once in a lifetime" property was costing them. They are paying less for the castle than the client I mentioned earlier had paid for one of his U.S. vacation houses.

It almost goes without saying that "good faith" exchanges are for the very experienced investors. This takes place when you have established mutual trust and credibility with your global property exchangers. These are professionals who believe in the win/win philosophy and who want to leave something on the table for the next property owner. It can be an exciting part of your investment portfolio.

PURCHASING FLOATING REAL ESTATE

Another very successful businessman loves the "owners' suite" purchased on one of the world's largest cruise ships. It is the ultimate vacation for one-to-four weeks, or even for a full year. When this man and his family members are not using this ship, it is in high demand as a "rental" by the cruise liner. There are many wealthy world travelers who, when cruising, will only stay in an owners' or penthouse suite. Incidentally, such luxurious suites often rapidly appreciate in value.

IN CONCLUSION

The exotic real estate market is here to stay. It is often the investment playground of the rich. With the advent of the Internet such properties are merely a "click" away from your consideration. If you are at this point in your investment career, I wish you happy hunting or happy sailing, as the case may be.

20

COMMERCIAL PROPERTY

———————◆———————

MORE THAN HOUSES

By the time I began purchasing commercial real estate properties, I felt I was a seasoned investor. From my own experience, and from what I have learned from sophisticated investor clients, I personally believe that you should jump into this arena only after learning the foundation principles of real estate investing.

Not all real estate is to be lived in. Nor is all real estate purchased to resell. Unlike home owners, most businesses continue to lease their office and retail space. Commercial property has long-term growth value and consistent cash flow as well. Think of the strip shopping centers in your area. Most of them have remained unchanged for decades, keeping the same tenants year after year. When they do have a vacancy, it generally fills immediately. Commercial real estate can involve retail shopping, office centers, restaurants, motels, and hotels.

Let us now return to the basics. As I have observed my very wealthy commercial investment clients, I have noticed a certain pattern developing. Let me illustrate: One client started his real estate investment company by buying a duplex. He later added a thirteen-unit apartment complex.

He then added three houses to his portfolio. When I next saw him, he had sold each of these and had purchased a twenty-one-store strip mall in an excellent neighborhood in Los Angeles. He is now retired, traveling the world and greatly enjoying his retirement years. At first he managed the strip mall himself, but now he has professional managers doing it for him. His retirement is secure, and the mall is mortgage free.

The pattern I often see with my clients evolves by taking the following steps:

Step 1: Experiment with smaller apartments and single-family houses, then

Step 2: Buy your first commercial property and learn the ropes, then

Step 3: Buy an even larger commercial property. Diversify your properties according to location. In most cases, you will have ensured financial security for yourself and your posterity.

The Importance of Using a Realtor – a Broker or Agent

Understanding one's limitations, both in knowledge and experience, is crucial to the commercial investor. Stakes are higher, market trends are more volatile, and occupancy rates all combine to make the use of a realtor almost mandatory. Both brokers and agents must be licensed in the state in which they do business; and this regulation is to the benefit of the investor. Realtors usually specialize in different areas, including those who focus their professional energies in the commercial arena.

When selecting a realtor, you would do well to choose

one who has been in the business for several years. The most informed realtors are those who are also active in their community, participating in their local Chamber of Commerce. They are constantly monitoring trends, market conditions, and specific commercial properties. Understanding rental rates, occupancy factors, and location advantages can make the difference between your success or failure. Select a realtor who stays informed of regional and national trends as well as local conditions. Even if you are a real estate agent yourself, utilize the expertise of others in your investing area. Paying commissions is a wise practice, both in buying and selling.

When retaining the services of a realtor, take your time. Choose someone who reflects your values, interests, capabilities, time availability, and temperament. This is someone who understands your needs as well as your short-term and long-term objectives. Test the relationship without making long-term commitments, and make sure your personalities mesh.

If you are able to find a broker or agent who "thinks" like you do, your collective energies will create a synergy that will pay dividends again and again. Two heads are better than one, and where one of you may be more sensitive to some issues, the other can provide complementary clarity.

My personal experience in using brokers has been very positive. Other investor friends have sometimes felt pressures exerted by a realtor. They are often motivated by commission, but if you find one who has your short-term and long-term interests in mind, you will not be pressured to buy a given property. Good realtors provide the pros and cons to a given transaction, then remain emotionally

detached so that you can made an unemotional determination. As a final note, retain the services of a broker or
agent who is imaginative and who can make an offer in your
behalf that may be ridiculously low. No offer is ridiculous,
especially when the seller is highly motivated.

RISK AND REWARD

It is essential to remember that commercial properties
often carry a greater market risk than residential dwellings.
I have seen office buildings that are 100 percent empty in
the wrong location, or that were built at the wrong time.
Commercial real estate values go up and down in cycles. Be
careful not to invest at the wrong part of the cycle. You can
calculate the cycle in a given area by the percentage of
commercial space vacancies.

One millionaire client of mine very quickly became an
ex-millionaire. He did this by investing his forty years of net
worth into one enclosed mall in the wrong location at the
wrong time. On more than one occasion, this client told
me that his three greatest mistakes were, 1) failure to
diversify his real estate holdings (Putting all of his eggs into
one basket proved fatal), 2) failure to have sufficient cash in
savings to tide him over for two or three years of hard times,
and 3) failure to structure his real estate ownership so that
it legally stood on its own.

In this investor's case, not only did he lose the mall but
also his home, his two vacations homes, and his personal
savings. He did not know how to structure an operating
"C" corporation to manage the mall, and a separate limited
partnership, or LLC to hold title to the land and buildings
on the land. Nor did he know how to use trusts and other
entities to insulate his personal assets from the potential
failure of his mall business.

IN CONCLUSION

Having expert legal counsel is essential for anyone going into the commercial real estate business. I own a small successfully-leased shopping mall that fits nicely into my own personal diversified mixture of real estate holdings, and I followed my own advice in the careful use of one corporation and three support limited partnerships to own various portions of the mall.

21

LAND DEVELOPMENT

❖

BUILD IT AND THEY WILL COME

Many investors shy away from undeveloped land because they see it as an ongoing expense. They see it as a high liability proposition with limited or no assurance of returns. The payments go out, the taxes go out, the insurance is paid, but where is the income?

Think about this for a moment. If there were any validity to these concerns, there would be no new development. To the contrary, you see new homes and businesses being built at every turn. What do the developers know that you do not? Perhaps, just as with foreclosures and other areas we have discussed, the difference is their knowledge and their active application of it, compared to what you currently know about land development. I say currently because even as you are reading this book, you are changing your level of understanding and your likelihood of success in this potentially lucrative business.

These deals are more complex than simple residential or business purchases. They generally take a longer period of time and involve more relationships. Still, it important to remember that complexity is your friend, not your enemy. Remember, if it were all easy, everyone would be doing it. The following are basics you need to know:

LOCATE THE GOOD DEALS

We will discuss speculation and the spotting of trends in a later chapter. For now, simply understand that deals are literally everywhere to be found. You want to consider where the population will be in three years, five years, ten years, and even longer. Often, specialized agents can help you with an educated forecast.

DEVELOP A SOUND PLAN

What do you see as the property's greatest use? Single-family homes? Hotel and services? Retail businesses? Offices? Future public use? Your vision will determine the kind of deal you must structure.

Let me illustrate this important real estate investing approach with my own failure. Because of what I was able to learn, it was actually one of my greatest success stories. I hope it will benefit you.

Many years ago, a friend told me of a choice farm that was twenty miles from the closest neighbor and thirty-five miles from the closest small town. I purchased this land for a song, knowing that someday it would increase in value and that I would get a good return. I ended up selling it twelve years later for less than I paid for it. In so doing, I learned the following lessons: First, purchase land for development only if it is in the path of growth. If development is not already in the general area, forget it. In my case, it will take 200 years or more before any development will reach that land. I also learned that land purchased in the wrong area is an alligator. I still had to pay property taxes, mortgage interest payments, and even insurance.

ADDITIONAL LESSONS TO LEARN

Contrast my experience as a young man in my twenties with those of a client of mine. He purchased a small five-acre fruit orchard from a family that had owned it for over eighty years. He told me that his secret was "buy the land, sell the lot." He then installed roads and utilities, carving the land into eighteen building lots. He gave one of the building lots to the original landowner and sold the other seventeen, making a profit of over $650,000!

Still, there are pitfalls to avoid. Another of my clients purchased six acres of farmland for development. The price was right, the market timing was perfect, and he reasoned that he could convince the city planning and zoning commission to rezone the property for higher density.

This last factor was his undoing. The city had been granting higher density housing, but their philosophy of growth had recently changed. Instead of having twenty-four building lots to sell to builders, he had only fourteen. Even further, the land was adjacent to a mink farm, and the city demanded that he build a block retaining wall around the entire subdivision.

By the time my friend complied with each of these "unexpected" requirements, he only broke even on the project. He felt he had escaped with his life and vowed to never buy land in that community again. Incidentally, it was the same conclusion other developers before him had reached. It was just sad that he hadn't done a little more homework before purchasing land in that area.

Another of my clients has a formula that reduces risk

while breeding success. He never pays for the land he is buying to develop. He simply enters into a profit-sharing arrangement with the landowner. He develops the land into lots by subordinating the original owner's interest to the bank that provides the development monies. He is happy to share the profits and is highly successful.

Still another investor, who is worth several hundred million dollars, has his own philosophy. In the late 1970s, while most developers were reeling with high interest rates and difficult times, this millionaire was busy buying up sections of land. He used profits from his "main business" and soon he was learning real estate. Because of the economy, he was able to get land for a song, and farmers and other developers alike were relieved to divest it from their holdings.

This investor gradually began to build a few homes in projected growth areas. He kept his costs down, then reduced his margin of profit, and all this while providing quality construction. Soon the economy turned, this developer grew into a builder, and now he builds 1,500 to 2,000 homes a year. Not only that, but his business became so successful that he sold his other business to devote all his time to his land-acquisition and building business.

The important thing is that this developer and builder purchased parcels of land during an economic period when others were getting out. He had cash flow from another highly successful business, and so he was able to buy land for cash. That made all the difference.

The point is, there is significant wealth to accumulate by purchasing the right parcel(s) of land at the right time and under the right circumstances. If you are considering this avenue of money-making, start out small as you learn the ropes. Above all, do your homework so that all of your investment bases are covered.

BUYING THE PROPERTY

The purchase of these properties often includes more complex deals, possibly involving several levels of relationships. For example, if you are building houses, you may include a general housing contractor in the deal. Doing so cuts or eliminates your costs of the actual development and allows you to share the ultimate profits.

Land syndicators are groups of investors who track and make offers on commercial property as speculators anticipating growth. By communicating and possibly teaming up with a group of this nature, you may be able to participate in the acquisition without incurring all the risk.

IN CONCLUSION

Purchasing land, either to hold or to develop, can be a very lucrative business. Timing is crucial, and the amount of debt you are obligated to carry can make or break your eventual profits. If you have payments during a period of nondevelopment or no revenue flow, make sure your available cash from other sources is adequate to hold you over.

Buying land and either holding it for a later sale or developing it for larger profits can enhance your wealth as few other real estate investments can. If you decide to develop the land, hire a professional developer who knows how to work with the municipality, as well as how to price out improvements such as utilities and curb and sidewalk. For those who are thorough and are schooled in the fine art of land development, millionaire status is almost ensured.

22

ESTATE AND PROBATE SALES

———————◆———————

WHEN SOMEONE DIES, SOMEONE ELSE PAYS

A person's estate includes the physical assets and financial worth they built up over their lifetime. When they pass away, their family is often left to dispose of unwanted assets and to pay the taxes and other costs due. "Probate" is the legal process that, under court supervision, distributes an estate to heirs and creditors. Without proper planning, estate taxes and inheritance taxes create an added financial burden on the estate and dilute its net value.

In this chapter, we ask the following question: How can you, as an investor, profit from probate sales? When these sales take place, the house and other real estate holdings in the estate are often sold first. This sale may even include the furniture and other belongings. If the children of the deceased are (1) established in their own homes, (2) if the family members live in a distant city, or (3) if there are several factions in the family who all get a portion of the proceeds from the sale of the estate, a wise investment may be made. Any one of these factors can increase the opportunity to get a great deal on real estate the family wants to sell. They are often very motivated.

Almost any real estate agent will tell you that probate

and estate sellers are among the most motivated of all sellers. Typically the children want to sell the family home, dividing the cash among themselves as quickly as possible.

There are two categories of such sellers:

Category #1   The sellers who are supervised by the probate court because the decedent used a will or died without a will.

Category #2   An increasingly large number of families using living trusts, so no probate is involved. Even so, the family is equally motivated to sell, and a purchase can be made even more quickly than with Category #1 sellers.

Watch the local newspaper and legal notices section of the business papers to locate this kind of seller. Periodic trips to the courthouse will help you locate Category #1 sellers, but not Category #2 sellers.

Part of the heirs' urgency is practical–with the aim in mind to pay off taxes or to split the proceeds from the estate. Part of their motivation is emotional if the family members want it all to be over so they can return to their lives.

The administrator or trustee of the estate must balance these needs and desires and dispose of the property in a way that is most beneficial to the remaining family members. If taxes are a burdensome area, the administrator or trustee has an added incentive to dispose of the property immediately.

A Caution, but Not a Concern

Many investors shy away from estate or probate sales. They have heard nightmare stories of how difficult it can become to clear a title. This is especially true when several children or grandchildren inherit the property. It is important to understand that this apparent caution also provides smooth sailing for the astute investor. The important thing is to have your attorney or title company be informed, then ready to track down the heirs so that the title can be passed on to you.

One Investor's Gold Mine

One of my associates has become a multimillionaire simply by exclusively focusing his energies in this area of real estate investing. He has literally become an expert in what he does. Always aware, he knows when to go to the courthouse the very day notices are posted. He carefully watches not only the notices and financial section of newspapers, but also the "Homes for Sale" and "Estate Sale" ads. He also knows of the small specialized newspapers that publish only legal notices without other news. From his experience, each of these is a rich source of referrals.

As another source of referrals, my friend contacts estate planning attorneys. He leaves his card with them. They know he is "for real," and that he is a quick source of purchases for their estate clients. Over the years he has become very close to three law firms and finds many of his best deals this way.

In Conclusion

Understanding estate and probate laws provides a rich source of potential properties for investors to purchase. These investors must understand that they are not exploiting persons in need of divesting properties. Rather, they are providing a much-needed "quick sale" source of funds for those in need. Although this avenue of real estate investing is not glamorous, it is often one of the best sources of creating wealth. Try it. My suspicion is that you will, in all likelihood, like it!

23

AUCTIONS

───────── ◆ ─────────

THOUSANDS OF AUCTIONS, EVERYDAY

There are many different kinds of regularly scheduled auctions throughout the country. These auctions are sponsored by city, state, and federal government agencies, banks, private auction houses, and even businesses. Many auctions include real estate and other items of significant value. Some of these auctions are "absolute," where any bid is acceptable. With others, those bidding must pay cash at the time of purchase.

If the person bidding is unable to pay cash, the item being auctioned goes to the next lowest bidder. In still other auctions, however, those bidding have from two to thirty days to complete the transaction. In some, they must register or post a deposit before they can bid, while with others there is no required deposit. Some auctions are "live," while others use a sealed bid.

The following are a sampling of the many types of auctions from which you can profit:

FORECLOSURES

We have covered these kinds of auctions in a previous chapter. They often take place on the courthouse steps and require payment at the time of bidding or shortly thereafter. To learn more in detail, reread the chapter on this lucrative business.

U.S. CUSTOMS

These auctions are held several times each year in many different locations. They are likely to include seized houses, cars, boats, planes, freight, etc. The largest of these may attract hundreds of people. Smaller ones may have fewer than a dozen bidders show up.

GENERAL SERVICES ADMINISTRATION AND MILITARY

The General Services Administration, or GSA, regularly auctions off government surplus equipment such as cars, trailers, post office trucks, computers, and other surplus items. These auctions may include properties formerly being used by the military. To find these auctions, check your local newspaper for dates and times. You can also call the GSA direct for the information.

U.S. MARSHAL

When a "drug bust" takes place within the United States, the U.S. Marshal's office seizes the property involved. They then sell this property to cover their expenses. This can include quality items such as houses, land, vehicles, heavy equipment, and household goods. Drug lords often live lavishly, buying high quality goods that may be purchased for pennies on the dollar.

SHERIFF

Items seized or found by local authorities are sold several times each year at a sheriff's sale. Automobiles are the most common fare, although there are always some surprises. Call the sheriff's office for dates and times of these sales.

NON-PROFIT ORGANIZATIONS, INCLUDING CHURCHES AND CHARITIES

When charities have property donated to them, they will often auction it off in order to generate revenue. Like some of the other auctions, the choices of property can range from vehicles to household goods to real property. As previously mentioned, you can sometimes develop a one-on-one working relationship with a charity and be first in line to buy, even before the date of an auction.

STORAGE UNITS

Although we cover the business of storage units later in this section, these are some of the most interesting and rewarding auctions of all. They may be operated like a "grab bag," where you bid on what is behind the sealed doors. Others may open the doors first and bid item by item. These auctions are always full of surprises and potential bargains.

VA AND HUD

The Veterans Administration and Department of Housing and Urban Development both guarantee loans. When a default takes place, these agencies are responsible for disposing of properties collateralizing these loans in an orderly manner.

Both of these auctions require a modest deposit prior to bidding. If you are successful in your bid, both agencies allow you a brief period of time to pay the balance due them.

You will have a certain number of days to view the property before the auction takes place. Call the local office of VA or HUD for further information. It may be one of the most profitable phone calls you will ever make.

OTHER REAL ESTATE SALES

In some cases, banks or other lenders may hold an auction to clear out their REO inventory. In some cases, these properties can be viewed in advance, while in other cases they can only be viewed the day of the auction. The auction house may rent a meeting room and have photos of the properties on the day of auction, with all bidding taking place in one location. Sometimes the properties may be auctioned on-site, with a literal caravan of bidders driving from one place to another.

As a hint, you would do well to get to know the auctioneers. Cultivate your relationship with them and they may lead you to properties to purchase. They may also lead you to other auctions to attend.

DEFINITE ADVANTAGES AND DISADVANTAGES

The primary advantage of buying real estate through auctions is that they are quick, exciting, and very educational. By attending auctions, you are able to learn comparable auction/market prices. In turn, you are able to purchase properties as an *informed* investor. Be patient, remain unemotional, and over time you will successfully bid on an incredible deal.

The "thrill of the auction" can also be a two-edged sword. Because of the excitement among the bidders, which is fueled by those in charge, many properties sell for market value or even above market value. Your calm, directed manner allows you to pounce when the deal is substantially below market value.

In spite of the peril of making an emotional purchase, attending auctions can be very lucrative. It can also provide a forum for you to meet other investors. In turn, these relationships can lead to an alliance where both of you may profit.

Learning to Bid Successfully

There are several steps to successful auction bidding. While this list is not exhaustive, it can be a point of beginning as you prepare to participate in your first auction.

Step 1: Learn which properties are to be auctioned. Take the time to visually inspect these properties, giving consideration to location, property condition, and other factors. These factors may include:

A. How much money will be required to put down at the time of auction?

B. How long will you have to pay the amount bid and close the purchase once a successful bid is made?

C. Does the property come with title insurance and a warranty deed, or is the title possibly clouded?

D. Is there any statement of condition, or warranty, on appliances, heating and air conditioning equipment, water softener, or sprinkler system? If not, in what condition are these items?

E. What is the condition of the home, itself? Sensitivity to paint, flooring, plumbing, peculiar odors, and cabinets and countertops is essential.

F. How does the value of the property compare with other properties in the area? Does it have curb appeal and what will it take to make it saleable?

Step 2: Once you have answered these questions to your satisfaction, determine what your highest bid will be. Make this determination based on market value, cost of repairs, and actual bidding price range. If possible, speak with realtors who have other house listings in the area. See how long those properties have been for sale, their comparative value, etc. A thorough investigation at this point can lead you to bid on only those properties that will lead you to a high rate of return on your investment.

Step 3: Once the auction begins, act almost disinterested. Never show your hand. Instead, lay back and watch the "action" as the other bidders reveal themselves. Only bid on a given property when it is about to be sold.

Once you state a bid, move the price up very slowly. This is aggravating to the other bidders, and has a tendency to put a damper on the bidding process. Be slow and methodical in raising your hand, and appear almost bored with the bidding process. Psyche has a great deal to do with auctions, and many bidders can be thwarted or discouraged by the investor who becomes an effective strategist.

In Conclusion

The aforementioned auctions are just some of the many that are available around the country. Once you begin attending them, you will get continuous alerts as to new auctions taking place in your area. Attend often and you will find some real bargains. These often become an incredible source for increasing wealth.

24

STORAGE UNITS

———————◆———————

EVERYONE HAS "JUNK" OR
EXCESS PERSONAL PROPERTY

Some individuals have more difficulty managing their excess personal property than others. These people are one of the primary markets that storage units appeal to. Others who rely on storage units are:

✓ People needing to store recreational vehicles, motorcycles, snow machines, boats, an extra automobile, etc.

✓ People downsizing their existing home

✓ Apartment-dwellers who have limited space for storage

✓ New residents needing a place to store their belongings until they get settled in

✓ People who live in gated communities with associations that have strict rules, disallowing storage buildings in their tenants' yard or open storage in their garage

✓ People who have suddenly lost a loved one, who must sort through years of accumulation

✓ City/county and state police, as well as other agencies

✓ Business owners needing storage space for files, supplies, excess equipment, and furniture

All of these people and more utilize storage unit centers, making a growing, unlimited market for this unique investment opportunity.

FORM FOLLOWS FUNCTION

How many of these storage units do you want to construct? If you find yourself considering making this unusual market part of your investment portfolio, there are several things you should know. If you are beginning with a raw piece of land, building storage units requires a minimal amount of construction. Unlike commercial office and/or retail space, these units require no finish work inside; not even paint! Except for the possible resident manager's living and office facilities, and an automatic sprinkler system, they require no plumbing. They often have metal roofs, as well as minimal landscaping and electricity.

The simple construction of storage units means low maintenance. The on-site manager spends most of his time signing new rental agreements, handling rent payments, overseeing security, and keeping the area neat and clean. A coat of paint every few years is usually the extent of normal required maintenance.

You will find that damage from storage tenants is practically nonexistent. Because their belongings are in "their" space, they have a pride of ownership. They are often aware of other tenants and develop an almost neighborly relationship with those who have rented units next to theirs.

One of the appeals to renters is the security offered. In a way, it is a well-managed gated community. Because of the presence of managers, and since it is well lit and secured with a gate, there is a definite sense of safety. Because storage units are usually located along a roadside, where there is ample traffic, it is not considered a significant target for theft. To the contrary, tenants feel very comfortable keeping their excess belongings in their locked unit.

Storage units simply "sit there" and make money.

Storage unit renters pay for the space, for the convenience, and for the security. It is unbelievable how long some people will keep their "used up" belongings in storage. These items often include family heirlooms, valuable equipment, or expensive recreational "toys."

As you consider the chapter you have read on developing land, keep storage units in mind. They take advantage of a powerful economic fact. Money flows to the bank month after month and year after year. For most renters, it is easier to pay a monthly storage fee than to deal with the items they are storing. Out of sight is truly out of mind, at least as far as their home and garage are concerned!

One client confessed to me his frustration with owning apartment buildings. He became tired of unclogging toilets, repairing holes in walls when tenants moved, replacing furnishings damaged by slovenly renters, evicting drug pushers, and receiving threats of physical harm by disgruntled tenants or friends of tenants. He gave up. He sold his apartments and purchased a 175-unit self-storage complex. Today, he is in investor heaven. Ninety-nine percent of his management headaches disappeared overnight. He cannot understand why everyone does not invest in storage units.

Now listen closely. One of my multimillionaire clients, who invests almost exclusively in storage units, recently confided a very exciting fact. Smiling, he proudly said, "Whenever I build another storage facility, I immediately double my net worth."

Upon further inquiry, my friend told me that he builds one new storage complex every twelve months. His latest complex cost a total of $3,700,000 for the land and all construction costs. If he chose to sell, he could easily dispose of it for a price of $8,000,000.

Three years ago, this same investor built another complex for a total cost of $1,465,000, including land. This storage complex is fully rented, and appraises for $3,200,000. This is over one-hundred percent profit! Given these two storage unit projects, is it any wonder that my friend almost exclusively uses this form of real estate investment?!

Without question, constructing a storage unit complex is a potential gold mine for an experienced real estate investor.

HIDDEN "RECESSION PROOF" GOLD MINES

Much like billboards, storage unit real estate investments are hidden opportunities. When the economy is strong, consumers buy more and more. Unfortunately, their homes are ill equipped to store their purchases. Therefore, they look to their nearest storage unit facility for relief.

Building or purchasing storage units is considered a recession-proof investment. It is impervious to economic conditions. Even in an economic down cycle, storage units are needed. Families choose this as an alternative to buying a larger home. Once they see the advantages of having an "off site" storage unit for their excess belongings, they become hooked. Making the monthly payment becomes as routine as paying a utility bill.

Often the perfect real estate investment, storage units generally require only one employee, a manager. The utility bills are minimal, and there is little or no upkeep on the units themselves.

What happens when a tenant doesn't pay?
Fortunately, when a payment is not made, you are not forced to go through legal maneuvers to evict the tenant. As per the terms of your rental agreement, you simply hold a "yard sale." Your manager puts a sign near the front entrance and maybe a small ad in the classified section of the local newspaper. They then dispose of the things in the delinquent renter's storage unit. Just the threat of a yard sale almost always brings the tenant in to bring his rental payment current.

For decades, only seven percent of the American public rented storage facilities. In the past several years, however, this number has multiplied four times to twenty-eight percent. One American family out of four now avails themselves of the "needed" opportunity of a storage unit. This trend is obviously rising, giving cause for sheer optimism for the storage unit investor.

Two Keys to Success
From my experience, there are two keys to success in the storage unit industry. The first, of course, is location. Having roadside visibility is the facility's best advertisement. The second key, related to the first, is to have a viable marketing strategy.

Several years ago, when my son and I built our first storage unit facility, we constructed it next to an existing storage facility. We knew going into our project that it had taken our competitor two-and-a-half years to reach 100 percent occupancy. This gave us a challenge we couldn't resist. We created an exciting name and motif, then spent the money to make it look like the finest storage facility in America, including a security system second to none. Not surprisingly, we were 100 percent occupied within seventy-five days! The cash flow has been outstanding and constant, and we are averaging an almost fourteen percent return on our investment.

My associate, James Smith, tells a similar story. "I have a very close friend and investment partner who purchased a storage facility. He expanded it to maximize his usage of space, and when he finally sold it, he walked away with a seven-figure profit on the transaction. Before this experience, he had never been able to make a million dollars in one year. In this instance, he did it with one real estate transaction."

In Conclusion

Including one or more storage unit facilities in your investment portfolio may be one of the wisest financial decisions you will make. With the right location and marketing strategy, there is almost no way you can lose.

If you are interested in an investment requiring minimal management, that has incredible cash flow, and that experiences steady appreciation, storage units are the answer. It is truly one of the most conservative and predictable real estate investments available.

25

MINERALS, OIL & GAS

———————◆———————

Have you ever wanted to be in the oil business or to own a gold mine?

Over the years, drilling and mining companies have repeatedly changed the manner in which they operate. At one time in our country's history, "wildcatters" went into wasteland areas and secured permits. In essence, they staked a claim that allowed them to drill or mine ore on government land. They also drilled or mined on their own land. They constructed the rigs and mine supports, dug the shafts, then drilled the wells. When precious ore was found, or when the oil gusher came in, the owners often danced all the way to the bank.

The first oil well I drilled on a piece of land I leased in Kentucky resulted in a "gusher." I knew I was set for life. However, six weeks later my dreams vanished when the gusher turned into a "stopper." I abandoned the well in the same manner thousands of other individuals have done with their wells and lost everything I had invested.

For many investors, the mine plays out or the well never does come in. To reduce the consequence of this happening, corporations and partnerships were formed.

These firms, with numerous investors, spread the risk as well as the profits.

Today, these companies often organize as a limited liability company (LLC), or a limited partnership. A large number of investors combine to each own a certain percentage of the well or mine. You are not forced to be a geologist or a mechanical engineer to profit from these joint ventures. You are not even compelled to participate in the actual mining or in the drilling of the well.

Purchasing a government land lease gives you the opportunity to make a profit without the extraordinary risks associated with speculative drilling or mining. Each year the U.S. Government auctions off mineral rights to thousands of plots of land for very low costs.

If this type of investment sounds like learning a foreign language, in a way it is. If you are interested in investing in this arena, getting competent professional assistance is a must. There are so many nuances, federal regulations, and product variables, that entering as a novice almost always spells failure. Take the time to be schooled in the area of your choice, then place confidence in a company, or investment tool, that spreads the risk. It can be exciting and very lucrative, if only you do it with all of your bases covered.

In Conclusion

Even with the enticements of immediate wealth and cash flow, this investment strategy is highly speculative. Over the years, it has been my legal experience that the majority of my client investors in minerals, oil, and gas have lost more than they have gained. At the same time, some of my client investors have made fortunes.

As part of a well-rounded real estate investment portfolio, I recommend this as an area in which to invest a maximum of ten percent of your investment dollars. Such an investment can be extremely profitable, although it must be approached cautiously and with thorough investigation. Finally, as my own experience as a thirty-one-year-old amateur investor illustrates, be prepared to lose it all.

26

BILLBOARDS

———————— ◆ ————————

**What has a small footprint
but carries a big financial stick?**

Imagine owning the ideal rental property. This real estate parcel is small and requires virtually no maintenance. This means no sinks, no toilets, no air conditioner, no heater, no washers, dryers, or dishwashers. In fact, it means no tenants! Best of all, it only takes up a few square feet of space.

Even with all of these restrictions, this ideal rental property often yields as much revenue as an apartment building. As a further enticement to invest in this revenue producer, you have almost no investment in the physical structure. You can use the rest of your property as you so choose. Does this sound like a dream? Believe me, it is very real. We're talking about billboards, of course, the real estate that yields the greatest revenue per square inch.

It has been said that the more things change, the more they stay the same. One thing that will never change is the need for businesses to advertise their goods and services to the public. As mentioned above, one of the most effective and time tested means of marketing is "outdoor advertising." This is commonly known as billboard advertising.

It has also been said that a business with no sign is a sign of no business. Remember the "dot com" era? Thousands of virtual new businesses used billboards to introduce themselves to the real world. Billboards that promoted business of a bygone era continue today by displaying advertising of a new business. This new advertising sustains positive cash flow for billboard owners.

UNDERSTANDING BILLBOARD ADVERTISING

One of the nice aspects to investing in billboards is the small financial commitment needed to do so. You are able to invest in one billboard at a time. Knowing this fact, where do you turn for immediate information about (a) the billboard advertising concept, and (b) demographic information about billboards as they relate to your area?

The answer is a only click away, on the Internet.

Not long ago, in order to learn more about my own area of Utah, I went on the Internet and typed in the words: **Real Estate Billboard Advertising**. The first of many pages appeared, the first one identified as "Salt Lake City Billboard Advertising." Intrigued, I began to read:

"Billboard advertising in Salt Lake City, Utah, is a great idea, as well as around the country. Over a million billboard advertisements every day are on their way." With this introduction, I read many things that pertained to this unique business opportunity–both from the vantage point of the advertiser as well as the real estate investor.

Regardless of which part of the country you are interested in purchasing a billboard in, the Internet will feature that area in detail. Once you have learned inside information about the business there, it is time for you to speak with individuals or companies that are doing business this way. I have found that regardless of the type of real estate opportunity you are examining, those already in the business are willing to share. In the main, professionals have a win/win mentality, knowing that they too have received help.

FIVE STRATEGIES FOR SUCCESS

Billboards are seldom if ever on the radar screen of the average real estate investor. However, if you were the average real estate investor, you likely wouldn't be reading this book. Even if you still feel "average," perhaps by learning and implementing several of the strategies of the billboard industry you can advance to the next level of successful real estate investing.

Notice: Don't be penny wise and dollar foolish. Always consult an attorney before conducting a real estate transaction.

STRATEGY #1

Buy, declare, and sell. When given the option, most people would rather own than rent — especially when in the real estate business. Before you erect a billboard, you should either (a) own the property, or (b) have permission from the land owner (usually in the form of a ground lease) to build on their property. The way to invest a limited amount of money on a property is to do the following:

1. Find a piece of property that would qualify for a billboard. A permit from the state and/or municipality is usually required.

2. Have the owner of the property "owner-finance" the purchase. You generally want to have the purchase

contingent upon your being able to receive the required building permit(s).

3. Once you have purchased the property, declare and file a perpetual sign/utility/access easement for the sign on the property.

4. Once the easement is filed, you can build the sign at any time. You can also sell or lease the easement to a billboard company if you don't want to be in the business of selling billboard advertising. Make sure to protect your investment by securing all of the necessary building permit(s) before talking to any billboard companies.

5. Sell the property subject to the terms and restrictions of the easement. If you choose to build the billboard before you sell the property, you can use your own billboard faces to advertise that the property is for sale.

6. Enjoy the fruits of your labors.

An Unlikely Success Story

One of my wealthy clients shares: "I stumbled onto this strategy when a property owner changed his mind after signing a ground lease with my company. The state informed me that the property owner had written them a letter stating that he did not want a billboard constructed on his property and that he had never heard of me or my company.

"I thought this to be very odd since this property owner had never told me this and because he had signed a contract with me just a few months earlier. So I went to this man's office and asked him why he had experienced a change of heart. I knew that I was well within my rights to still erect a billboard on the property, but I wanted clarification.

"The property owner informed me that he had decided to sell the property and that in his opinion having a billboard on it might make it more difficult for him to sell. In response, I asked this man if he would sell the property to me. He said that he would and agreed to owner-finance the transaction. I closed on the property three days later and built the sign the following week.

"This sign had four faces, two of which had been sold three months earlier after I signed the ground lease with the property owner. On one of the remaining faces, I posed an ad that read: "This Property for Sale by Owner." I also included my phone number.

"The ad produced two or three phone inquiries a day. Since I was selling the property for a premium, most of the buyers laughed or never called back. Still, I kept the names and phone numbers of those inquiring, just in case I decided to lower the asking sales price. Within two weeks, I had a contract with a prospective buyer. However, because he could not obtain financing, the sale fell through. By this time, I had already leased the other two faces on the sign and had removed the "For Sale" ad. So I bought a small "For Sale by Owner" sign, stuck it into the ground next to the road, and had another contract within two weeks.

"In this instance, I agreed to owner-finance the property on a one-year note. I then had the primary lien holder sign off on a 'wrap.' That way, I wasn't obligated to pay off my note on the property before reselling it. The property, along with the easement, was then conveyed to the new owner. This meant that once the property was paid off (within twelve months), the ad revenue produced almost a 100 percent profit!"

STRATEGY #2

First right of refusal: Sometimes, property owners don't want to sell their property or provide you with an easement. In this case, you may opt to sign a ground lease and pay rent in order to have the right to erect a billboard on their property. However, if you have a first right of refusal clause built into your contract, when the owner does sell the property, you're first in line to match any offer acceptable to the owner. Once you purchase the property, start at number three on Strategy #1 (above).

A GREAT SUCCESS STORY

One of my millionaire associates shares the following: "The first billboard contract I entered into (containing a first right of refusal clause) was on a little country road. That road is now in the middle of the fastest growing city in the county. When the property owners decided they wanted to sell out and move further into the country, they called me. Since they already had an offer to purchase on the property, I asked the buyer if he would still be interested in the property if I declared a sign easement prior to his purchasing the property. Let me add parenthetically that if he would have had a problem with the easement, I would have purchased the property, myself. I would have then declared a sign easement, then resold the property to someone else.

"As it turned out, this man agreed to purchase the property subject to the easement. As a result, the property owner signed a contract to sell the property along with the "to be declared" easement to the buyer. Prior to closing, I signed an easement purchase agreement with the property owner. I then hired a surveyor to draw up the metes and bounds of the easement. When this was accomplished, I filed the easement with the county. Once again, I obtained another rent-free billboard location."

STRATEGY #3

Sublease: If you have an advertiser, but no billboard space:

✓ Find an available billboard your client would like

✓ Secure a contract to lease the sign (preferably for less than your advertiser will pay you). Make sure the billboard lease contract contains a noncompete and noninterference clause in it

✓ Enjoy cashing the check each month for being a middleman in the deal

One of my clients shares: "I have a wonderful renter who pays me a check at the beginning of each month. He needed a billboard in an area where one could not be built. So I signed a contract for $1,100 per month. I then signed a lease on a billboard (which I rented) for $500 per month. Even though I am obligated to pay rent, I had no out-of-pocket expense in generating a $600 per month profit. Next year, my client's rental rate increases by fifteen percent. Even so, my rent will remain the same. It is a very lucrative investment."

STRATEGY #4

Anticipate the future. This sounds difficult to do, but in the billboard business, it a vital strategy to profitable growth. The following are ways to stay ahead of the curve:

1. Talk with local and national home builders in your area.

Ask them where they plan to build and if they need any directional signage

2. Investigate the areas where signage is needed for possible billboard sites

3. Secure a location using any of the above three strategies or one of your own

4. Secure an advertising contract

5. Build your sign

6. Enjoy the quick return on investment, or ROI, of the billboard business

Another of my associates relates the following: "One of my favorite clients is a national home builder who uses extensive directional billboard advertising. He likes to build in outlying areas where I am often able to obtain permits to build new signs. I learn where a new development is being planned, at which time I sign a contract with a property owner along the proposed route to the new development. Once I have a permit to build the sign, I go back to the home builder and invite them to sign an advertising contract. I then build the leased sign, beginning an immediate revenue stream.

STRATEGY #5

Study newly built-up locations. You can often become the benefactor of someone else's efforts. When a new billboard is constructed, there is frequently a perfect opportunity to build another billboard on either side of the new location. Remember, most of the time a permit is required to do this. Obtain the local sign ordinance and state regulations to learn what the rules of engagement are for new billboards in your market area.

One of my wealthy clients states: "A competitor of mine purchased a trailer for a business owner so that his property could qualify for a billboard permit. Upon learning of the recently issued permit, I found a one-acre parcel of land that was for sale. It was located near the site where the new billboard was to be constructed. I made an offer for the property, which was contingent upon my receiving a permit to build a billboard.

"Once the permit was issued, I closed on the property and began the process of carving out an easement on the property and reselling it. Since the market price of the property was less than the property I had sold earlier in the year (which was about two miles away from the present site), I went to work. I called several of the inquirers from the other property. These were individuals who were looking for less expensive property.

"My strategy worked, and I was in possession of a signed contract within one week. I have since sold the property subject to the restrictions of the easement, and I have a contract for advertising on the billboard that is scheduled to be built later this month."

In summary, the above five strategies are not theoretical. Each of them has been used successfully by clients and each is proven to be profitable. Remember: To succeed in *any* business requires effort. But with patience and persistence, you can reap both the short-term and long-term profits this unusually lucrative and trouble-free real estate investment strategy provides.

Businesses Really *Do* Advertise!

Improved real estate is defined as any land upon which improvements have been made. Billboards certainly qualify as an improvement on a piece of property. People advertise, plain and simple. One of the least expensive types of advertising is to use billboards. When the economy is good, people advertise on billboards. Then, when the economy goes bad, billboards are an inexpensive way for a merchant to continue to advertise. The cost per "viewer" is very low. Many people drive the same highways day after day, allowing the appeal of what is being advertised to embed itself in their buying considerations.

As a money-making investment, one of the attractive features of billboards is that the owner is not compelled to deal with destructive, uncaring tenants. There are no improvements to repair, such as toilets, draperies, or carpet, and there is no grass to maintain. It is a very "clean" wealth enhancer, with little or no maintenance headaches.

Many times, merchants who advertise on billboards are nationally known. Because you may have billboards in several states, merchants often rent all of these in one block.

Owning a billboard is an unlikely yet very profitable real estate investment. Once the billboard is constructed, the approximate cost of $30,000 has been expended. The billboard owner can then lease the sign space to a tenant, receiving from $1,500 to $4,000 per month in rental income. It is the perfect "cash flow" real estate investment for those who take the time to understand local markets, traffic, and trends.

Let me share a concluding true story. Several years ago a man living in Dallas, Texas, noticed an unused billboard at the side of a road. It was old, but it was still in good condition. Strangely, it hadn't been used for some time. Inquiring through the state highway department, this man learned that this billboard was "orphaned." That is, it had been abandoned by whomever had built it in the first place. Upon making formal application to acquire the billboard, the state of Texas basically allowed him to "adopt" it for free.

With ownership in the sign, this man advertised its space and rented it out for $3,000 per month. Intrigued by his good fortune, the man used the revenue he received to lease additional billboards. He now has several billboards that he subleases out to merchants. His lease payment on each of them averages $500, and he subleases them for between $900 to $1,100.

On one occasion, this investor inquired about purchasing a billboard that was owned by a man who had recently died. In speaking to this man's widow, and inquiring about the possibility of purchasing the sign from her, she replied, "Absolutely not." When the man inquired why she was so adamant about not selling, she answered: "Because I put my kids through school on that billboard, and now I'm retired on its income. I'm keeping this investment forever."

IN CONCLUSION

As these actual experiences illustrate, billboard real estate investments can be uncommonly profitable. It is a quiet cottage industry, a niche investment area that can produce cash flow from very reliable tenants or merchants. Although it is a "difference" investment strategy, in that it is widely considered, it *is* almost risk free.

In good economic times, as well as in bad, merchants

rely on highway traffic to feed their businesses. Again, start out slowly with one billboard. Watch this segment of your portfolio bring a smile to your face every time you pass the billboard as well as every time you deposit the rental check into your account.

27

"OTHER PEOPLE'S MONEY" AND THE CONSORTIUM

———————◆———————

To make your business grow exponentially, use other people's money (OPM).

A central truth many growing business owners will learn is this: to grow quickly, you must go outside your own resources. Most investors simply do not have enough liquidity to do everything needed in order to achieve optimal growth. To progress to some of the advanced strategies presented in this section, you will ultimately need to consider bringing in other investors or providers of funds.

In reality, you use OPM or "other people's money" every time you borrow money from a bank or use a credit card. However, this chapter is meant to bridge an inevitable gap. This is the gap between the expectation of "no money down" real estate and the reality that many highly profitable deals will be greatly facilitated by going beyond your own personal funds. It may even take you beyond your bank line of credit. When this occurs, you will begin to consider OPM.

Building a stable of investors is a key to growing

exponentially. Build your plan and promote your vision. To accomplish this, participate in your local chamber of commerce as well as in other community functions where successful local business people are in attendance. In other words, network. Have a clear idea of what you are about and what you need. As you gain a level of comfort with some of these new associates, invite them to consider participating in a profit-making investment with you.

Two Very Creative Success Stories

One of my extremely wealthy clients conceived a brilliant plan. His program worked, and now he is a multimillionaire. Even though he did not have sufficient money of his own, he knew how to buy "fixer-upper" real estate. On one occasion, he spoke with a physician neighbor about his idea. The doctor got together four other doctors from his clinic, and the five of them formed a relationship with my client. He proposed what he felt would be a better return for the doctors than money in an IRA, stocks, or in a bank savings account. The group brainstormed, formulated a viable plan, and now all six are millionaires. The following plan forever changed their lives:

- ✓ It was agreed that my client would search and find real estate deals
- ✓ The five doctors would provide all the investment dollars for the venture
- ✓ My client received a 1/3 ownership interest in every deal he found for the group
- ✓ My client both hired and supervised the repairs of the rental homes and apartments for the doctors

According to my last conversation with this client, his partnership with the physicians had lasted eight years. He had every reason to believe that it would go on for at least another eight years. You might say, "Why would doctors do such a thing?" This is a valid question. They had confidence in my client. They trusted him and felt that his interest percentage was well worth it to them. They considered it a win/win situation. No doctor in their clinic could work full-time, or even part-time, to find good real estate investment deals. Nor could they supervise the fixer-uppers, the negotiations and sale of the property for a profit, and then start the process all over again.

The second story involves one the clients I referred to earlier in the book. He was the one who purchased a house and a duplex, both in the wrong location. This client learned his lesson, and soon formed a real estate development company. He surrounded himself with two seasoned managing partners, and together they hired the most competent real estate attorney in his area.

This client was soon putting together syndications, or limited partnerships. My client and his associates had an American contact in Saudi Arabia, and soon they were making trips across the world to fund large real estate projects here in the states. The last time I heard, they had funded several large apartment complexes, two large office buildings, and six acres of raw commercial land. His plan was to build a hotel on the land. Both my client and his partners became millionaires, doing so with OPM.

RETAINING CONTROL

You can include specific investors for specific projects, or pool their resources and create a group project. The key is for you to retain control over the project. After all, it is your knowledge that makes the deal possible while reducing or eliminating your financial risk in the deal. In the chapter on Hard Money, we will explore another way to utilize OPM once you obtain it.

Finding new and ongoing sources of OPM is a key element to the continuing growth of your business. As you consider the different strategies in this section, bear in mind that the cost of the money you use is insignificant in comparison to the profits you will be making.

THE POWER OF MORE THAN ONE

Using the concepts discussed above, you will likely discover two or three investors with whom you enjoy working. These are persons, or groups, who trust you and are ready, willing, and able to fund your projects.

Using your knowledge and skills as a real estate investor, as well as a manager, you can create a deal in which you have no cash invested. You work hard, maintain your integrity, then allow this investment group to share the project's profits with you.

A consortium is a group of people with money who want to see their money grow faster than interest rates or stocks will routinely allow. These individuals are often willing to take some risks to see this take place. They must trust that you know what you are doing and will wisely steward their investment. Remember your mission statement. This is where your reputation for honesty and integrity will repay you a thousand times over.

It is essential for you to remember that you are entering into this relationship from a position of strength, not with your hand out. You are the deal-maker, and they need you.

You have the real estate investment knowledge and you will make a profit using their money. They will thank you and ask you if you will repeat the process, perhaps for years to come.

In Conclusion

Learning to utilize the strength of other people's money, or OPM, can create wealth exponentially. This is a condition where numbers, or dollars, accumulate more rapidly than they otherwise could have grown. The two key factors to being successful in real estate with OPM are (1) competency in acquisition, repairs, and selling, and (2) having personal authenticity or trustworthiness to steward the money honestly. Millionaires are made many times a day, and more often than not with the help of OPM.

28

HARD-MONEY LENDING

◆

MAKING MONEY WITH HIGH-INTEREST LOANS

If you have good credit, you undoubtedly shop for the most competitive rates and terms before borrowing money. Millions of people with poor credit can only borrow "expensive" money. These funds come from high-interest loans that are known as "hard" money.

Before exploring this area, let us define what we mean by "hard" money. These are loans that are highly secured: First, by placing a mortgage on the property itself; second, by requiring a high equity stake in the property so it is virtually impossible for the lender to lose his money; and third, sometimes requiring other real estate or assets to be pledged as collateral for the lender.

Who are the lenders of these loans? If you are a mortgage broker, they are your outside investors. (more uses for OPM!) Becoming a mortgage broker entails different requirements in each state and is generally required if you are providing loan services to others. These investors, like those in your consortium, want to earn more return with their money than traditional investments allow. They also want to experience less risk than the real estate investment group, or consortium, is willing to accept.

Depending on state laws, you can provide endless loans for them to fund with interest rates that vary from ten to eighteen percent. These mortgage loans are often secured by a forty to sixty percent equity in the property. As a broker, you earn from one to ten points, depending on the loan funded.

Who would ever pay that much money for a mortgage loan?

1. People who have had some bad breaks, but who own a property with substantial equity
2. Elderly people who cannot get a loan to repair something on their home
3. Other retirees with great credit, but with incomes that fall below standard loan criteria
4. Families who are suddenly left with a broken down house (a "wholesale" property) and cannot get a bank to even consider giving them a loan to fix it up until after the repairs are made

In short, there are millions of people who can use the kind of loan you can provide. Many successful "investors" will make these loans because (a) the return is so high, and (b) because doing so evolves into a regular retirement income.

FROM THE VANTAGE OF THE BORROWER

Even though you might borrow directly from individual investors, giving them an equity stake in a property in return for generous terms that allow you to quickly make a profit, doing so can be a sound investment strategy.

The investor, or money loaner, makes a quick profit while you have the funds you need to quickly close on a hot property. This is especially true with auctions and foreclosures, where having the ability to close in twenty-four hours can make or break the opportunity to complete the deal. Remember the chapter on OPM. It is not the cost of the money that makes the difference. Rather, it is the availability of funds with which to do the deal.

DESIGNING A SUCCESSFUL "PACKAGE" TO OBTAIN FINANCING

When seeking hard money as a borrower, it is essential to prepare a thorough presentation. Organize your needs, as well as the opportunity. Include graphs predicting cash flow, photographs of location, an artist's rendering of the building you are constructing, or whatever other nuances exist in your proposed real estate package. Bind it in a nice folder and give the appearance of sound investment strategy for the investor.

The following items should be included in your funding package:

1. A title page, which states:
    A. The amount of money needed
    B. Your name and address
    C. Your lending source name and address
    D. A brief mission statement of the project
2. A well-written, one-page business plan for the project
3. A cash flow projection — one year and five year, or projected profit if a quick turn-around is expected. A contingent plan if the property does not sell as anticipated

4. Your resume, including personal financial statement

5. A brief description of the collateral you are offering for the funds to be received

6. A copy of your personal credit report

7. A copy of your two previous year's personal tax returns

8. Several personal & professional references

9. Projected ROI, or return on investment for the lender (Include benefits to the lender for granting the loan)

10. A list of past real estate projects and history of these projects, including profits (or losses) made

Even though you are going after hard money, rather than a conventional loan for your investment package, it is wise for you to treat your request similarly. When a private investor is able to see your intent, as well as your organization and full disclosure, he will be much more likely to grant you the funds. As an alternative approach, you could ask his requirements for granting the loan. Providing more information than has been requested will always play to your advantage.

THE TYPE OF INVESTOR/BORROWER RELATIONSHIP TO FORM

It has been my experience, as well as the experience of successful "borrowing" clients, that there is often the tendency to invite the investor into the project as a partner. Even though this appears to his advantage, it can often create problems within the project. Most partners have their own agenda, their way of conducting the business of a project, and their expectations for managing, selling it off, etc. Such partnerships, therefore, can turn sour.

Accordingly, it is generally wise to take money with a fixed rate of return to the investor. If you are absolutely convinced that taking on a partner is the way to go, by all means limit your relationship to a specific real estate project. You can evaluate your relationship with the lender one project at a time, always giving yourself the option of continuing the project.

One of my clients, who has borrowed hard money again and again, has followed this rule exclusively. In his words, "By allowing my investor partner to participate on a project basis, rather than as an owner in my business, I have set up an 'easy in' 'easy out' relationship. It is easy for both of us to maintain the relationship, as well as to exit it should our conditions change, or should our ability to 'partner' be inhibited."

Regardless of the type of relationship you have with an investor, always consult your attorney to make sure the terms and conditions of the loan are properly stated and documented. The "hard money" source can be very profitable, and easy to manage; but be wise as a fox in entering into such a relationship.

AGAIN, AS THE INVESTOR

In hard-money lending, you can be the provider of funds yourself or a coprovider of funds with some other investors. On the other hand, you can even be a "user" by borrowing from others in order to make quick deals.

One client shared with me a simple, direct ad he regularly places in the financial section of his local newspaper. He shared with me that his average return is more than triple the rate he could get on his money if he invested it elsewhere. His little ad simply states:

Have Money to Lend–
Immediately Available.
Call 000-000-0000.

What a retirement this client has built off one simple ad idea!

A VERY STRONG CAUTION

If you are in the business of loaning money, and if you have extended family members who know this, then you will inevitably be approached by them for a loan. Family members, often as a last resort, make this request out of desperation. They may not qualify for a standard bank loan, or they may be starting up a business. Even more frequently, they may have a "dire circumstance," which requires funds.

Whatever the reason for this request, the outcome is almost always a disaster. I know many clients who have been sensitive and responded by providing funds. These same investors almost always end up writing off the loan, forgiving it for the sake of the relationship. More often than not, such an arrangement leads to "distancing," discomfort, and even bitterness.

Many of my clients, when faced with this dilemma, have come to the same conclusion. As one of my clients expressed to me, "I have made it my policy that when family members request a loan, I tell them I can't afford such a loan . . . and I can't. The *relationship* can't afford a default. Instead, if I have the funds, I simply give them what I can, with no expectations for a return. I call it a 'gift,' and it has proven to be a sound solution. From sad experience, I have found that this is the best way to preserve the relationship."

Still another of my clients grants relatives the loan, and has them sign the papers with an "adjusted" lower interest rate. He then silently writes off the loan without the family borrower knowing. This solves any future problem for my investor client, although a default will still cause the borrowing family member to distance themselves from their "loaning" relative. It is a double-edged sword when family is concerned, but it is solvable in this manner.

IN CONCLUSION

Finding hard money is often a wise strategy for the borrower. It is similarly good for the lender or investor. Working together can be a win/win arrangement and can allow creative deals to be made, which might otherwise not be made by a conventional lender.

Whether you are the investor, who loans hard money to others, or the borrower, who wants to catapult his growth exponentially by acquiring additional cash, be thorough in your approach. Hard money is a sound investment strategy as well as a good source of funds for financing a new project.

29

THE PAPER BUSINESS

———————◆———————

BUYING AND SELLING PAPER: YIELDS OF TWENTY TO FIFTY PERCENT OR MORE ON YOUR MONEY!

When a financial institution needs to raise money, they often sell off some of their outstanding loans. These loans are referred to in the business as "paper." They sell this paper to another financial institution at a discount. Perhaps they have a large number of personal loans under $5,000. They may sell off all or a portion of these loans at less than face value in order to raise the revenues they need for further growth.

Why would a financial institution sell a loan to another bank or institution for less than its value?

Do you remember my mentioning money and time? Money does not have a fixed value. Its value changes over time. A dollar bill is worth 100 cents today. It was worth the same amount ten years ago and will be ten years from now. But that is the physical value of the bill or coin. The investor mind-set is to think of money as a product, one that generates revenue all by itself.

THE TIME VALUE OF MONEY

The thing that changes over time is money's *usable* value. I previously discussed how many times a year you can "turn" a dollar. The time value of money is expressed in percentages, or as the present value of a future stream of income. One way we see the value of money is in the form of interest accrued from borrowing the money. We all know it costs money to borrow money. The difference is the money's value to its owner, which in this instance is the bank. You will pay its value if you want to borrow it.

When a loan is made, the interest not yet paid is unearned. It is not earned until you make the payment. Money is said to have a "future value." The bank that loaned the money received points at the beginning point of the loan. This bank has generally received principal and interest funds along the way. Another reality is that $100 received ten years from now is not as valuable as $100 received in one year. In fact, to an investor the "present value" of $100 to be received ten years from now may only be worth $5 to $20.

A loan is a marketable commodity. But for another bank to purchase it, they will determine what its future value will be. If that future value is $10,000, they will need a reduction or "discount" in order to entice them to purchase it. Why? Because of their calculation of today's present value of a future receivable or a future stream of income.

A "DISCOUNT" DEFINED

In reality, a discount is simply "interest in reverse." Although it describes reducing the selling price, it is based on the return the purchasing bank wants to make on the loan it is purchasing. Different lenders will have different requirements for how much of a discount they must have.

Assume, for a moment, that the selling bank has $5,000 in principal left on a $10,000 yield to maturity loan. They could sell the loan for $5,000 and still get back all their original principal. Or, depending on the prevailing interest rates, they might sell the loan for $6,000 and get their principal back with an additional $1,000 profit. The purchasing bank would get a loan that pays off $4,000 profit by the maturity date. A little quick math will tell you that a $6,000 investment by the purchaser will give them an additional $4,000 profit by the maturity date. The borrower never pays a penny more on his monthly payment. In fact, he may never be aware that his loan was even sold.

YIELD IS WHAT MATTERS MOST

The purchasing bank's annual yield will depend on the remaining loan term. If, in the previous example, the loan is paid off one year later, the buying financial institution is still satisfied. They invested $6,000, then had this amount returned to them along with a year's worth of interest. If the loan is paid through its full term, they get back a total of $10,000, which amounts to a profit of 40 percent. Of course, if the payments are made over a period of time, the rate of return decreases.

THIS IS THE POWER OF DISCOUNTED PAPER

And, it is not limited to banks! As an investor, you can buy and sell discount paper yourself. You can easily learn to factor the time value of money, which is figured in four parts:

✓ **Term (number of payments)**
✓ **Monthly payment amount**
✓ **Interest rate**
✓ **Present value or principal amount**

If you know any three of these parts, the fourth can be easily factored using a financial calculator such as one manufactured by Hewlett-Packard or Texas Instruments. You use the same information to compute mortgage loans and payoffs when making offers on property. Receiving tutoring with these calculations is invaluable and can increase your efficiency.

WHERE DO YOU FIND LOANS?

You can run ads in the paper, visit local businesses, and utilize these techniques in your arsenal as you are buying and selling homes. Here are a few people who will jump at the chance to sell you a loan at a discount:

✓ People who have sold a house and hold a mortgage
✓ Individual holders of first or second mortgages
✓ Mobile home retailers
✓ Used car dealers
✓ Other investors
✓ Thrift and financing institutions that provide equipment and personal property loans
✓ Retailers who sell their own in-house paper at a discount to other institutions

Do you remember the investor mentioned earlier who bought and sold mobile homes by using these techniques? He would purchase a used mobile home for, say $7,000, put it on a subdivided, one-quarter acre with a well, electricity, and septic tank, adding an investment of approximately $7,000 more. He would then sell it for $30,000, with $1000 down. He would hold the mortgage for twenty years. He had a ready group of investors who would buy the first five years of these mortgages for $12,000.

The first five years of payments generated roughly a twenty-eight percent yield on their investment. In the final sum of things, this investor got his money back to do another deal. Amazingly, he still had fifteen years of payments to look forward to! The last time we saw each other he had over sixty of these deals completed, with each deal paying for the next. He was within months of getting his first big "payday" from his "bank."

One investor keeps an ad running in his local paper, which says: "I buy notes and mortgages. Immediate cash to you!"

This investor is making a handsome return on his investments. His experience is just one example of how creative you can be when you use all the tools in your toolbox and do not lock yourself into doing only one or two kinds of deals.

IN CONCLUSION

Learning to buy and/or sell "paper" can be a very lucrative portion of your business. Financial institutions are shrewd, experienced, and profit-seeking. When they establish a procedure of buying and/or selling paper, money is to be made.

As the above example illustrates, a niche money market can be made for someone who writes paper, then sells it off at a discount. The key is to understand the "present value" of money and how receiving immediate cash flow can enable you to grow your business that much more quickly. This is a sound investment strategy and one that is repeated thousands of times every day of the year.

30

REITS
"REAL ESTATE INVESTMENT TRUSTS"

———————◆———————

THE FORMALIZED INVESTOR GROUP

We have discussed the concept of including other investors in real estate dealings, either to fund the deals (as in a consortium), or to fund *your* deals through hard money lending. A more formalized approach, and one that reduces the risks associated with any real estate or mortgage investment, is the Real Estate Investment Trust.

A Real Estate Investment Trust, or REIT, is an entity that buys, develops, and usually operates its own income-generating real estate. These properties may include apartments, office buildings, shopping centers, hotels and motels, and manufacturing and warehouse facilities. Investors can participate in professionally managed portfolios, and use REITs as a means of diversifying their stock, bond, and other personal investment strategies.

WHY IS A REIT SO DIFFERENT FROM A CORPORATION OR A CONSORTIUM?

The major difference in these entities lies in how they report and pay taxes and how they "pass-through" the taxes on their earnings to their investors. A traditional "C" corporation, for example, must pay taxes at the corporate level first, then distribute any remaining after-tax profits to its investors as dividends. As a private investor, you are responsible for paying taxes *again*, this time on the portion distributed to you as a dividend. Investors in these companies now pay taxes on the dividend distributed to them from the already taxed corporate earnings. This, in fact, amounts to double taxation on the very same income. A corporation, then, typically retains a large share of the earnings for its own use.

On the other hand, the great news is that the main purpose of a REIT is to make money and pass the profits back to the investors without the "double tax." In fact, as we will see, REITs are required by law to pass at least 90 percent of their profits back to their investors. The tax bill for these revenues is passed through to you, and the REIT is not liable for taxes on any of the money they pay out "pre-tax." Because of this, more money ends up in the hands of the investors. Your profits are taxed only once, based upon your own personal tax rate.

A LONG HISTORY OF MAKING AND SAVING MONEY FOR INVESTORS

As described above, REITs are used by investors to avoid corporate double taxation. Because these unique entities distribute their income to their investors, they are not taxed at the entity level.

During the 1930s, this advantage was taken away, once again creating double taxation. There were first corporate, then individual taxes for each investor's share. Following World War II, the demand for real estate funding skyrocketed as returning servicemen created the largest housing boom in our country's history. Finally, in 1960, President Eisenhower signed the Real Estate Investment Trust Tax Provision. The purpose of this provision was to spur real estate investment dollars. This important law once again made REITs what are referred to as "pass-through" entities, eliminating the double taxation problem.

WHERE WE STAND TODAY

The law has remained much the same since 1960, with a few important enhancements. First, while the Tax Reform Act of 1986 was seen by some as the end of the easy and lucrative "good old days" for real estate investors, REITs were given additional leeway to not only invest in, but also to *manage* their own properties. Before this time, REITs had been required to use a third party management company. In 1993, they were further strengthened when, for the first time, Congress allowed pension funds to also invest in REITs.

THREE KINDS OF REITS

There are many varieties of investment trusts, but they are all essentially associations of individual investors, or "beneficiaries." These associations have joined together, pooling their resources for investment purposes, with a designated "trustee" or management team.

REITs fall into three categories:

1) **Equity REITs.** The vast majority of REITs are directly involved with investing in, owning, and operating their own income-producing properties. Most of their

revenues come from rental income. In fact, unlike many of the other real estate strategies we have discussed, REITs must be oriented toward "buy and hold," managing their portfolios for long-term profits, instead of buying to sell.

2) **Mortgage REITs.** A very small number of REITs are structured to lend money directly to real estate investors or homeowners, or to acquire discounted loans for long-term payback value.

3) **Hybrid REITs.** These REITs do exactly as their name suggests, both lending money and investing in and managing real property.

A REIT is governed as a security, similar to the way stocks and bonds are regulated. Even so, REITs have a number of advantages over more commonplace securities. For example, all REITs are required by law to pay dividends. Unlike partnerships, a REIT cannot pass its tax losses to its investors. There are a number of federal and state laws that govern how these trusts must operate: Generally a REIT MUST:

✓ Have at least 100 investors or beneficiaries
✓ Be managed by a board or by trustees
✓ Have fully transferable shares
✓ No more than fifty percent of the shares can be held by five (or fewer) investors
✓ Seventy-five percent of the assets MUST be real estate investments, and seventy-five percent of the REIT's income MUST come from real property or mortgage interest

✓ Less than twenty percent of the trust's assets can be in stocks

✓ Ninety percent of the annual gross income MUST be distributed to shareholders (investors) in the year it is earned

Basically, these characteristics boil down to an entity that primarily holds long-term real estate investments as its main source of income. It is one that pays out almost all of its taxable income to its beneficiaries, shareholders, or investors.

I have previously described the major benefits of REITs. These include a diversified portfolio, lower risk investments, and a single level of taxation.

Again I ask, have you figured out the major drawback? It is simply this: REITs can only keep ten percent of their earnings each year. While this is good news for the investors, it means that the trust will often be raising new dollars for additional investments.

When the real estate boom cycle of the 1980s burst and values dropped across the country, an increasing number of REITs began raising new dollars through public stock exchanges. For many investors, the spreading of the risks and the opportunity to participate in the commercial real estate market (by pooling their money with other investors) was just what the economic doctor ordered. As a result, publically traded real estate companies became a much more common feature.

Using the combined financial leverage of its members, a REIT can acquire and profit from significantly larger deals than a single investor (or even a small consortium)

could ever hope for. The pooling of resources of 100 or more small-to-moderate investors can generate huge investment benefits. Do you remember the chapter on storage units? One millionaire client of mine builds a storage complex, gets it rented out, then sells it to a REIT at fair market value. I've never seen him get less than a seventy-five percent profit over construction costs, and often the profits exceed 100 percent.

WHAT IS IN IT FOR YOU?

The best way to describe a REIT is as a "total return investment." You stand to earn significant returns and steady, long-term revenues, so your return on investment (ROI) continues to increase, quarter after quarter, with no further investment required.

IN CONCLUSION

REITs provide the following benefits to the investor:

- Ongoing dividends, high yields, and increasing dividend amounts. According to industry watchers, REITs consistently earn more than the rate of inflation, and more than you can earn with a savings account
- Liquidity. Unlike most real estate, if you need to cash in your shares in a REIT, you can do so quickly
- A diversified portfolio with professional management and minimum risks
- Significant tax advantages over most other approaches

Although Real Estate Investor Trusts are not for everyone, they carry huge potential for the investors who choose to participate. As your business grows, consider expanding your reach by participating in a REIT. It does not need to curtail your other invest-ments. Consider it a part of your ever-expanding millionaire portfolio of profitable opportunities.

FINE-TUNING YOUR
REAL ESTATE INVESTMENT BUSINESS

31

DESIGNING A SPECIFIC PLAN FOR YOUR BUSINESS

◆

A BUSINESS PLAN IS ESSENTIAL

When most of us think of a business plan, an image of boardrooms and corporate planning are the first things that come to mind. Most small businesses don't have a business plan. Could it be that the lack of a solid plan, or the inability to create one, is a major reason that most new small businesses fail?

A business plan serves many purposes, including the following:

✓ To formulate and project the growth of a business

✓ To clearly define what a business does

✓ To state the purpose of a business, and the vision and mission as the owner (or board) sees it

✓ To identify markets and opportunities

✓ To spell out how a business will approach these markets and opportunities

✓ To identify the strong points that give a business the "edge"

✓ To identify the key participants . . . the "dream team" that makes it all work

✓ To map out strategies for business growth

✓ To keep a business on track

✓ To help other interested investors see the potential and gain confidence in your business

These are just a few of the purposes of a viable business plan. Yet, as observed before, small businesses generally do not put great importance on a well thought-out plan. If they do, it is often on a "back burner" of their list of priorities.

"It's All in My Head!"

Home-based business owners frequently make this mistake. I suppose there is something about a brick and mortar business that somehow makes it more "real." Doing a business from home is almost akin to a hobby. At least, that is often how it is treated. Owners know what their business is, right? After all, they have it inside their head. Just ask them.

Every business needs a business plan, and every *successful* business has one.

For most of us, the entire business plan concept is about discipline. I am sure you know persons who spend weeks planning for their annual vacation, yet who try to keep the details of their businesses in their heads. They never bother to write down their plan. It is as if they are afraid that doing so somehow becomes binding. Lacking the discipline to follow through may be a part of their reluctance to write it down. Or, putting a plan in writing may make them feel that they cannot change their minds without somehow "failing." Even if this does not describe your approach to doing business, perhaps you can relate to this kind of thinking.

Why do we experience these confusing emotions? I believe it is because we naturally treat anything in writing as being *real*. It is like the person who will "believe it when he sees it." This person tends to believe what they see in black and white.

For the *best* answer as to why you need a business plan in your business, I will turn to an old saying that explains it better than any I have ever found. During my career I have seen the truth in this edict make more than one person uncomfortable. It is simply this:

When it is written down, it gets done!

We all have dreams and hopes, wishes and goals. Changing a dream to a goal begins the moment we commit the dream to writing. Dreams are related to hopes, and hopes do not require substance. In fact, by definition a hope has *no* substance, and only because of faith and belief does a hope differ from a wish or a fantasy. A hope has some degree of faith behind it, while a wish is trusting in Lady Luck, or fate, to see it become a reality. A dream is something we long for, desire, think about, and hunger for. When we write our dreams down, they take on a tangible nature in black and white. They become real. They immediately become goals.

GOALS AND YOUR BUSINESS PLAN

Having an effective business plan requires understanding the nature of goals. Why cannot goals simply be in your

head? While they certainly originate there, they get tangled
up with your dreams and hopes, your doubts and fears.
These are all in an endless wrestling match for control over
your life. For most people, goals are sometimes at the top of
the heap. At other times, they become slippery and slide to
the bottom.

Your goals can positively define and direct your life,
followed by your hopes and dreams. While each of these
empower you, your goals have the benefit of substance, and
can keep your life on track. Doubts, fears, and other
emotions will most often serve to keep you from reaching
your full potential. Having clear-cut goals is perhaps your
best resource in your quest for success.

Goals have certain clearly definable characteristics,
which separate them from the rest of the information in the
brain. These goals can provide the edge in your life if you
learn to utilize their power.

Four Characteristics of Goals:

1. **Goals must be conceivable.** You must be able to think
    of a goal. It must have some specific nature to it. Putting
    it in writing is one aspect of goal-setting, but clearly
    defining goals requires focus and thought. First and
    foremost, your goals need to be specific. Wanting to
    "grow your real estate business" is not really a goal,
    anymore than eating good food, driving a nice car, or
    living in a luxury home are. If you don't have a specific
    idea of where you are going, how in the world will you
    know when you have gotten there?

    Our definition of such words as *grow, big, nice,* and
    pretty all change with time and circumstances. Likewise,
    wanting to be the Queen of England is a nice fantasy;

but unless you were born into the British Royal Family, there is no conceivable way for you to achieve it. Make your goals specific, clear, and concise. Now you have a conceivable goal that can be attained.

2. **Goals must be believable.** "If you can conceive it and believe it," Napoleon Hill said, "you can achieve it." Wanting to double your business is getting closer to home, but if your business has not grown more than five percent a year, do you really believe it can be done? It is all well and good to shoot for the stars and hope you will hit the moon — as opposed to shooting for the barn and hitting the mud — but do you believe you can achieve this goal in the first place?

   This is where your study and preparedness, as well as the guidance you will receive from your personal trainer, mentor, or other advisors, will be invaluable. You will grow in confidence and empowerment, and you will begin to conceive of where your business can go. You will also believe that you are equipped to take it there.

3. **Goals must be achievable.** In an age where communication is instantaneous, people are living in a space station above the earth. We have cut months of journeying down to three hours of air travel. The envelope we label "achievable" seems to be boundless. Even so, one of the greatest success-killers is setting goals that are beyond the realm of probability. You will notice I didn't say *possibility*, because arguably almost any goal is possible. The real test lies in your ability to achieve the goal. It does not matter if you are considering your actual or perceived abilities.

Perception Becomes Reality

Someone once said that "if you think you can, or if you think you cannot, you are right." Your mind and your emotions will play a tug-of-war with each other, talking to each other constantly. You can "see the light," and get excited about what you can do. Even so, your mind — in its own perceived logic — will go to work on your willpower to bring you down. Through your study, training, and experiences, you are able to raise the bar on your perception of your abilities, of your reality. You make your mind, emotions, and will get in line so they are working in concert with each other instead of at odds.

Two Caveats

Making a significant goal is as important as making it achievable. To be ultimately successful, you must learn to do both. Your goals should make you stretch. As you know, when muscles are stretched and pushed, they grow. Admittedly, if you are paralyzed by the fear of speaking to people, calling one seller might be a major goal for the day. The success you have in reaching your goals will give you the confidence to set even higher goals.

Making the first offer, or making ten calls a day, etc., are believable and achievable goals you can accomplish. They may also put you outside your comfort zone, although not outside your true abilities. It is by setting and achieving goals that you gain a sense of power and begin to glimpse your personal potential.

Don't get caught in the trap of "analysis paralysis."

This caveat is given to those who get lost analyzing whether or not a goal is too big to achieve or too small to help them grow. Is it precise enough? Do I really believe it, or not? Should I recompute my projections, figures, math? These are the questions you might ask yourself

As a rule, make goals that are big and that are a little outside your comfort zone. Still, do not make them so overwhelming that you get discouraged. Once this is accomplished, move on to number four.

4. **Goals must be measurable.** Finally, when you have set some goals that are both achievable and believable, the time has come to plan. For many, this process is the key link in the chain of accomplishment. Plan your step-by-step approach to reaching your destination, your goal. Although there are no perfect analogies, this one comes close.

Close your eyes for a moment and consider a make-believe journey. Imagine that you have decided to travel across America in order to "see it all." You have seen the travel shows, and you know millions of people are doing the things you want to do. You have a new car, a full tank of gas, and you believe that with sufficient cash you have the ability to make such a trip. So you lock up your home and drive down the road and out of town. However, you have no plan as to where you will spend the first night, as to how many days driving will be involved, or how much the trip is going to cost. You have not taken the time to break your trip into segments. You don't have an understanding of the time involved, the road construction you will encounter along the way, where you will stay each night, or what you will do once you reach your destination.

Several hours out of town, you begin to realize that your journey is bigger than you had anticipated. You sleep in a rest area for the night, then turn around and return home the next day. And all the while, you wonder where you went wrong.

PLAN YOUR WORK, THEN WORK YOUR PLAN

This is the crucial step, the missing link for most people in their own life as well as in the life of their growing real estate business. It is too easy to *not* take the time to plan a strategy and to figure out the steps that need to be taken to reach the destination. Without a plan, however, most ventures are doomed to fail. Because you did not get into business to fail, you need a viable business plan.

Only with a plan can you keep your eye on the goal, while taking the individual steps necessary to reach it. Only with a plan can you implement the strategies that will lead along the upper path to success. However, just as knowledge without application has no power, you must have commitment to achieve your goals.

A business plan is *not* the result of having clearly-defined goals for your business. Clear, concise goals are the result of having a comprehensive business plan.

Through the "fleshing out" process required to create a thorough plan, you give your goals both *form* and *substance*. As you explore your strengths and weaknesses, as you honestly look at your hours, your finances, your market and other factors, you gain clarity. As you consider the added benefit of a personal trainer and live training to help you grow in knowledge and confidence, you prepare for optimal success. As you go through the process of creating a comprehensive business plan, you will find the plan, itself, gives life to your goals.

You will see your goals begin to take on substance because the business plan itself validates them with reason and factual information. It puts in print what you want to achieve and makes your objective real in your mind. By using your business plan as your guide, you will much more likely stay on track until you achieve your goals

Take time to carefully think through what you want to achieve in your business. Consider every aspect, and let your business plan guide you as you set goals you fully intend on achieving. Then commit to the achievement of these goals.

Your business plan is your road map to business success, and it will help you meet your objectives. Having a plan for your business *now* will get you on track and keep you on track. You can always change your plan as you go along. After all, it is not written in stone. If you find certain market sectors more appealing, or discover that they seem to better fit in with your overall strategy, pursue them. If you spot a trend or a new hotspot in your area, you can add this to your plan. After all, it is *your* plan.

"Wouldn't I just do the same things, anyway?"

Perhaps; but without a business plan it is extremely easy to become so sidetracked that the new opportunities and strategies have the negative result of getting you off-track. When this occurs, the benefits are outweighed by potentially derailing or delaying your ultimate goals. While a business plan cannot eliminate every possible problem you encounter in your business, it *can* help you eliminate many of the difficulties that can be avoided ahead of time. In addition, it can provide alternative strategies for dealing with other obstacles as they arise.

What is involved in writing a business plan?

There are sound computer software programs to help you organize your thoughts. Still, you can use this book as a brief guideline to help you get started. Review your goals with your personal trainer, staff, family members, and advisors. Do this to ensure that your plan, and your business, stays on track. I recommend you draft a thorough business plan, as is prudent for any business. Although some parts of the plan may not seem necessary, do them anyway. Remember, creating wealth through real estate is not your hobby or pastime. It has become your *business*. Perception really does equal reality. Make it real for you, do it right, and the wealth will naturally follow.

Your business plan should include:
1. **The Executive Summary.** This is the first section of your plan, and should generally be no more than a page or two in length. It summarizes the *who, what, where, when, how, and why* of your business. *Who* you are, *what* you do, *where* and in which markets, *when* (time frames and projections), *how* (overall strategies for accomplishing your goals), and *why* (mission, vision, and goals). Use these as guidelines more than subject headings. Your business goals should be clearly and concisely stated in a paragraph within the Executive Summary. This section is the distillation of your entire plan and

should be reviewed and revised regularly as your business evolves.

While to this point in this chapter I have chosen to speak generically, it is now time for you to give focus and clarity to your plan. You have likely read Section II, feeling more comfortable with one type of real estate investment cookie cutter than another. While you may ultimately branch out into several of these areas, for now it is wise to become an expert in the one that best "suits you" at this time. If you take the shotgun approach, which could easily happen by having too general a plan, you risk floundering and will likely give up. Instead, choose one path, learn everything there is to know about that path, and pursue it. In all likelihood, you will find it lined with gold!

2. **Description of your business.** This is where you write, in detail, the facts that make your specific real estate approach unique. And it IS unique because it is *your* business. Include sections about you and your strengths, about how your office will be set up, needed equipment, expected hours of operation each week, and areas of focus. Who else will be involved? What are their duties? What is your business philosophy, your statement of purpose? Identify your short-, mid-, and long-range goals. Include your resume or bio and appropriate contact information. If you ever end up using other people's money, or OPM, you will be thankful you were organized at this early business hour.

3. **Description of the industry.** What do you know about the business? Write this section as though you were explaining your business to a complete novice or to another investor.

4. **Description of your market.** What areas are you going after? What kinds of values are in each? Who will you be primarily dealing with? Owners, sellers, agents, bankers? What trends do you see? How will you take advantage of these trends? What strategies are you going to utilize? Why? Who do you see as your competition?

5. **Description of your finances.** What kind of rates of return can be expected? What operating capital do you have? This section is less narrative and more analytical than the others. Construct a balance sheet, including income and expenses. Figure your expenses, and do a break-even analysis. What will it cost to run your business, and how long do you anticipate before closing your first deal? Explain how the business will affect this, and what your plans are for the revenues you are planning to receive.

For many, this is the most difficult part of making a business plan. To openly review and analyze one's finances is way outside of most people's comfort zones. Nevertheless, this is business, and business is about money. This defining moment may best be met face on by hiring a tutor, a real estate coach, or an advisor.

Looking honestly at your finances may reveal surprises . . . often good ones. Knowing where you stand as you begin your business gives you a critical benchmark for success in your business. Make sure that you don't skip this important step in your overall plan.

YOUR BUSINESS PLAN IS A "LIVING TOOL"

Once you have completed your plan, and have reviewed it with your adviser and committed yourself to seeing it through, you are miles ahead of the vast majority of other small business owners. Although this simple process takes time and involves specific thinking processes, it is invaluable to you and to the ultimate success you will achieve in your business.

Your plan is a *living* part of your business, not a static document confined to a notebook on a bookshelf. Use it like you would any other tool and refer to it often. Just as a pilot corrects his course continuously to allow for changing winds and speed, update your business plan as often as is necessary. By doing this, it will continue to be a living guide for your business to help ensure that you achieve your goals. Creating a business plan is a sound first step to ultimate success.

Once you have completed the creative process, you will be empowered to achieve your goals. This occurs when you commit to your business plan, then use it!

32

STRUCTURING YOUR REAL ESTATE OWNERSHIP TO PROTECT YOURSELF FROM LAWSUITS

◆

It has been my pleasure to spend most of my professional life teaching clients how to protect their assets. From my own experience, as well as from those of my multimillionaire clients, no area is of greater significance.

Home ownership is one of the great societal goals we dream about. Still, in today's complex world, personal ownership can easily become a nightmare reality. As a real estate investor, ownership is a liability, plain and simple, both from a legal and tax standpoint. On a personal basis, I have found no justifiable reason to ever have real estate in my own name. The ego boost of seeing my name on the public record has long since passed. In fact, from a legal, tax advantage, and liability viewpoint, I advise my clients to never hold property in their personal names. Society has become too litigious. Because of this, there are a number of ways to structure your legal "entities" so that your name does not appear on public records as the owner.

A Primer on Entities

Entities are the legal "structures" used to separate and protect the financial, taxable, legal, and other important areas of our lives and businesses. There are many entities I recommend to my clients, such as trusts, corporations, limited liability companies, etc. Often these legal entities work together. One simple entity frequently used for real estate is a land trust. This instrument gives you complete control as the primary beneficiary, but the public records only show the name of your chosen trustee. At the same time, your trustee must follow your directions regarding the trust, leaving you in control of its disposition.

Though this instrument is used to provide privacy, it does not provide the greater lawsuit and asset protection available through limited partnerships and limited liability companies when a serious plaintiff is about to sue you. Many well-intended advisers have seen their clients loose assets in a land trust. As a precaution, go for the greater protection and see an expert asset protection attorney.

(The following excerpt is taken from my book, *Cover Your Assets: Lawsuit Protection,* Crown Trade Paperbacks, New York).

How Business Assets Should Be Held

I met an old friend on the street who knew I did a lot of asset protection and estate planning work. He told me of a friend of his who had developed a successful new specialty — suing business owners. To my surprise, when I asked whether this man practiced any other kind of law, he told me he wasn't a lawyer at all. He was a former business owner who found he could make more money suing others than he ever had as a businessman. In just two years he was awarded five homes and commercial buildings, and he was about to seize a sixth.

Within our litigious society, many people have become adept at suing. These "professional plaintiffs" often commence lawsuits with only a slim chance of winning. Even so, they know that defendants will often cut a deal and quickly settle a lawsuit rather than devote the time and expense necessary to go to trial. These professional plaintiffs will target business owners with plenty to lose, and a judgment against a business can result in the loss of the business real estate. Similarly, non-real estate investments can also be lost to a judgment creditor. Insurance may not protect you if the insurance policy contains exclusionary clauses or if the amount of liability protection is inadequate.

THE PLAN

Years ago, armed with an MBA degree and contemplating law school, I taught some undergraduate university courses in finance, tax, and business. I must confess that I taught that there was no reason for the complexity of multiple corporations: My pitch was that one corporation would do the trick, even if it operated many different businesses. Today, I wish I could contact every one of my students and confess that I was wrong.

If you want to protect yourself in today's sue-hungry society, you must learn to design multiple entities to ensure your financial survival. You must always anticipate that litigation, liens, wrongful termination actions, seizures, levies, and EPA actions can financially destroy you.

Carefully review the nature of your business and

professional activities. Can you logically divide that business or professional activity into two or more separate entities? Without appearing trite, the more entities the better. While the process of dividing up ownership of your assets may confuse your banker, it can definitely save your assets.

Real Estate Used in Your Business

Business real estate should generally be owned by an entity other than the business itself. In most situations, you can gain substantial asset protection by separating the real estate ownership from the entity that is using the real estate. If owning and leasing real estate is your business, the real estate should be owned by other entities such as limited partnerships or trusts. The business operation itself should be a separate, distinct legal entity such as a corporation.

I have a client who owns three apartment buildings. He has legally placed the buildings into three separate limited partnerships. If one limited partnership is sued because of faulty wiring in the apartment building it owns, the other limited partnerships and their assets will be protected. Sometimes, additional protection is provided by structuring the ownership in this way, then leasing the buildings to an operating corporation to manage them. Many attorneys believe this approach provides enhanced protection.

In our law firm, my associates and I generally recommend to clients that real estate used by a business should be owned by a separate legal entity, then leased to the business. For example, we recommended to a group of eight Dallas doctors that they transfer title to their building into a limited partnership owned by the eight doctors and their families.

This was accomplished. The limited partnership then leased the building to the physicians' medical practice, which was incorporated. In the event of a malpractice suit against the doctors, the real estate owned in this manner was now generally immune from loss. Had the doctors done nothing, a malpractice lawsuit could have resulted in the loss of the entire medical complex.

ACCUMULATE AND PROTECT

Most business owners in this country are vulnerable to this kind of loss. They spend much more time accumulating wealth than on protecting that wealth. The written lease between the entities is critical. We generally advise our clients to structure the lease so that all liability flows to the tenant. This means that your business or professional corporation has the task of maintaining the premises, providing upkeep and repairs, insuring the property, and defending it in case of a lawsuit. The tenant should be fully responsible for all defects, and he/she must agree to be solely responsible for making the real estate safe and usable by all who come on the premises. This is our rationale:

A woman who had tripped and fractured her hip was awarded $600,000 in a suit against the people associated with the office building in which she was injured. The court was then forced to decide who should be required to pay the damages. The owner of the building was absolved of responsibility because the property had been leased under a tightly drawn agreement that made the lessee responsible for the maintenance of the property. It also provided that, in the event of any legal action, the lessee would be obligated to indemnify the owner.

In a similar case in Louisiana, the owner of real estate used by a fishing camp was not liable when someone fell through some steps and was injured. The lease held the owner harmless for any hazard of which he had not been notified, and the tenant had assumed the responsibility for maintenance and upkeep. The lease further provided indemnification to the owner.

LEASE PROTECTION

Generally, a lease is one of two types. The first type contains clauses designed to protect the owner (lessor) of the real estate. The second type is designed to protect the tenant (lessee) by transferring many of the responsibilities back to the owner. It is dangerous to simply use a lease form that you purchase at an office/supply store. It is well worth your time and expense to have a lease agreement drafted that protects you if you are either the real estate owner or the tenant.

What happens if both the lessor and the lessee read this book? In all likelihood, the lease they sign will not favor either of them. Rather, they and their attorneys will negotiate each major issue, and will draft a lease that reflects their negotiated agreement. For example, the lease might provide that the property taxes will be paid by the owner of the property, but that the tenant will maintain the insurance and provide a copy of the insurance policy to the owner.

Some lease forms provide a list of key issues such as property taxes, insurance, window breakage, wiring, and painting, as well as major and minor maintenance. Space is provided where those signing can check whether the tenant or the owner will be responsible for each type of expense.

My general approach with clients is that real estate used in a business should be held in a limited partnership. This is because of the advanced lawsuit protection afforded by these entities.

While another option is titling the real estate in the name of a separate corporation, this strategy may create major tax problems. Real estate could also be placed into the living trust of the less vulnerable spouse, or given to the children or conveyed to a children's trust for their benefit. This last arrangement has the additional advantage of allowing the rents and lease income from the real estate to go to the children, often reducing the overall income taxes owed by the family.

POTENTIAL ENVIRONMENTAL DISASTERS WITH YOUR REAL ESTATE

Laws concerning environmental hazards add an entirely new area of potential liability to owning real estate. On one occasion, I was teaching a seminar in Florida. A man approached me and said, "Jay, I have a piece of property downtown. It is appraised for $8 million, and has a $1 million bank loan on it. I'd be glad to give it to you for free."

I soon learned that a former owner had dumped toxic chemicals in the back of the property, contaminating the soil. There is now a potential $12 million EPA fine, and under EPA laws, the present owner of the property is liable for the fine even though it was a previous owner who dumped the chemicals. The bank even refused to foreclose on its $1 million mortgage because, as the new owner, it could become liable for the $12 million fine.

Another man left a job with a large corporation to go into business for himself. He purchased an old gas station in Magna, Utah. His goal was to use it as an auto mechanic shop. He didn't realize that there were three old two-thousand-gallon gasoline tanks buried beneath the land. Because these tanks had leaked, federal law requires him, as the property owner, to clean up any toxic wastes. The cost of cleaning up the property will be far more than his original purchase price of $40,000, and he faces additional state and federal fines. Had he purchased the property in the name of a corporation, limited liability company, or a limited partnership, in all likelihood he could have avoided personal fines and the probable bankruptcy he now faces.

What could these two businessmen have done differently? The general rule I follow is to acquire property either in the name of a corporation, a limited partnership, or a limited liability company. Doing so will provide substantial protection in the event of just such problems. I will never acquire real estate in my name, my wife's name, or joint ownership, or in my wife's or my living trusts. Never! Instead, we acquire properties in the name of an entity that will protect our family from loss.

HOW OTHER BUSINESS ASSETS SHOULD BE HELD

More than ninety percent of the businesses I examine are poorly structured. Imagine my surprise when I found that my new clients, four hotel-owning brothers, had structured their hotel business correctly. They came to me because they were being sued, and they were very matter-of-fact about it.

"We knew that the hotel business is dangerous and that this would happen one day," remarked one of the brothers. "That is why we decided to set up our hotel operation this way."

The four brothers set up a corporation to operate and manage the hotel and employees. That corporation held few valuable assets. The hotel building and land were put into a limited partnership, the ownership of which was divided between the four families. The limited partnership then leased the hotel building and land to the corporation.

I congratulated the brothers for seeking out advisors who would suggest advanced planning to guard against future lawsuits. "Oh, no," said one brother, "we did a lot of reading and studying on our own and decided, ourselves, how we should set up the hotel operation. When we told our advisors what we wanted done, they opposed it. They told us that Americans didn't usually structure businesses this way. We decided we would do it anyway."

Thank goodness these brothers had done just that. Although the lawsuit, plus other financial problems, put the corporation on the verge of bankruptcy, the valuable hotel building and land were insulated and protected.

We generally set up hotel operations so that the land and building are owned by a limited partnership. The hotel operation, itself, is managed by a separate corporation. The limited partnership leases the land and building to the operating corporation. The hotel business is a potentially dangerous business. If someone is injured or killed on the premises, or if an employee files a wrongful termination lawsuit, a judgment would usually be rendered against the hotel corporation. The operating corporation could even declare bankruptcy without affecting the limited partnership that owns the hotel building and land.

Marriott's Maneuver

In 1992, the Marriott Corporation divided their operations into two corporations. Marriott International

Corporation owned trade names, reservation and franchise systems, and its business operated the hotels and service businesses. The Host Marriott Corporation, as successor to the existing company, owned the hotel properties and other assets. This second company assumed Marriott's $2.9 billion debt.

Marriott's reorganization was a positive move toward modern asset protection, using multiple entities instead of one. In sum, they separated the operating entity, which was the most likely to be sued, from the less vulnerable asset-owning entity. I wondered what took them so long to implement this strategy. They could have learned a thing or two many years ago from the four brothers who owned just one hotel.

PROTECT ONE BUSINESS WHEN ANOTHER IS SUED

Two businesses should never operate together without legally separating the entities. In fact, even if you operate only one business, you should separate the components of that business in order to protect yourself against a possible lawsuit. At a recent meeting of the Chicago Dental Convention, I encouraged those attending to use one professional corporation for the practice of dentistry and a separate and distinct corporation for a dental laboratory with which they may be involved.

A lumber store I advised is also structured for effective asset protection. The lumber store real estate, including the land and building, is owned by a family limited partnership. The lumber store itself is operated by a corporation. The manufacture of trusses is conducted by another separate corporation.

Why all this effort? The lumber store could be a

defendant in a wrongful termination action, or perhaps be sued because a defective can of paint blew up, or even because a twenty-five-cent gum ball caused an illness. We did not want a lawsuit against the lumber store to close down the truss manufacturing business. Nor did we want a lawsuit against the lumber store to result in seizure of the land and building. Most importantly, because of the danger of truss manufacturing, we did not want a judgment against the truss business to deplete the lumber store or result in seizure of the land and the buildings.

One ski resort with six ski runs formed a separate corporation for each ski run. One group in New York City has formed over twenty corporations. Surprisingly, each corporation owns two taxi-cabs.

A POSSIBLE SCENARIO

The following illustrates how I would work with a typical client. Let us assume for a moment that a Mr. Jones owns three businesses. These consist of a car wash, an income tax service, and a home remodeling business. In addition, he owns the car wash building and a separate building for his tax service.

To provide Mr. Jones with the proper protections for his businesses, I would set up three separate "C" corporations to manage them. I would then create two limited partnerships, with each of them owning one building. I would next create a lease between the car wash corporation and the limited partnership that owns the car wash building. Finally, I would execute a second lease between the income tax service corporation and the limited partnership that owns the building where the tax service is located. Under certain circumstances, I might use a trust or even a limited liability company in lieu of a limited partnership.

The profits of each operating business will probably be paid as salary to the owner who operates the business. Two of the operating corporations will also make lease payments to the limited partnership that owns the building in which it is housed. This structure offers a significant income tax advantage to a family desiring to pass income along to children to be taxed at their lower tax rates.

Remember, however, that children younger than fourteen are taxed at their parents' tax rates. For example, if Mr. Jones has teenage children, he can make them the primary limited partners. Within this structure, the lease income will be taxed to them. The money could be accumulated for their college educations or other special needs. A one-year lease allows for a greater deductible lease payment than does a three-year lease, which must have a lower annual lease payment.

Consequently, if the needs of the children are great, Mr. Jones will want to use the shorter lease period for the leases. Even if the partners are not the children, for superior asset protection Mr. Jones may wish to utilize shorter lease terms. This will allow him to maximize the transfer of funds from the operating corporation to the limited partnerships. This is advisable because the limited partnership has superior lawsuit protection for cash and other accumulating assets than does the corporation.

A Basic Rule to Follow

Although many entities are involved, the basic principle of asset protection is simple: Separate the operations that are vulnerable to lawsuit from the assets to be protected. Many professionals expect the day to come when accountants, attorneys, and financial planners become vulnerable to lawsuits, themselves, for poor advice. This could happen each time these professionals recommend the traditional approach of setting up one corporation to operate the business and hold all assets, rather than structuring businesses with multiple entities for maximum protection.

An Analysis of the Law

The courts will generally consider two corporations being set up as separate and distinct. They will agree that one is not merely the alter ego of the other, especially if all corporate formalities are maintained independently within the two separate entities. The mere fact that corporations share the same officer and directors, or even the same owners, will not automatically destroy the separateness of the corporations. Nor will it cause the courts to pierce the corporate veil.

Complete disregard of corporate formalities for your multiple corporations will, however, cause multiple problems. The corporate veil will be pierced where a corporation is created or used for an improper purpose, or where the corporate form has been abused. Many factors are considered, including whether the corporation formalities have been disregarded, and whether the corporation was undercapitalized. Other factors may include whether there has been an intermingling of corporate and personal funds, whether there has been payment of corporate dividends, whether there has been siphoning of funds by the stockholders, and whether the debtor corporation was insolvent at the time.

The courts may also consider whether the same office or business locations were used by the corporation and its individual stockholders, or whether there was an absence of corporate records. They may also consider whether there are non-functioning officers or directors, whether there was a diversion of the corporation's funds or assets to non-corporate uses, whether there was failure to maintain an arm's length relationship, and whether there is a domination and control of the corporation that it is indistinguishable from the shareholder.

If two or more corporations or other entities are used, each must comply precisely with state laws. State and federal tax returns should be filed, meetings should be held, and advertising and promotion should be done in the name of each separate entity. Ask your attorney to help you design a checklist of the procedures that you must follow to maintain the separateness and independence of the two legal business entities. Remember that a corporation requires much more stringent compliance than does a limited partnership. For example, a limited partnership has no requirement for monthly, quarterly, or annual meetings.

In a case involving breach of contract, two corporations were sued even though the contract was with just one of them. Testimony revealed that the two corporations were very closely tied together, and that correspondence for both corporations was sent to just one of the corporations. The court found that because the corporations were so intimately linked, they were in essence acting as one contracting entity, and that the corporations' affairs were indistinguishable one from the other.

In the words of the court, if there is evidence of

"blending of identities, or a blurring of lines of distinction, both formal and substantive, between two corporations or between an individual and a corporation, factors such as identity of shareholders, directors, officers, and employees, failure to distinguish in ordinary business between the two entities, and failure to observe proper formalities, are important. The separateness of the two entities disappears. Therefore, each corporation is liable for the acts of the other."

LAW CONSCIOUS AND LAW ABIDING

It is important to carefully set up your business structure. However, as the above case illustrates, it is equally important to adhere to every letter of the law.

In a similar case, an insolvent corporation was sued by someone who leased property from it. Because the corporation was insolvent, the plaintiff also sued a related corporation that had deeper pockets, arguing that the corporations weren't really separate entities and should be joined together in the suit as one entity. The court disagreed. In order for the second corporation to be liable for the first corporation's debts, it reasoned, the plaintiff must establish that "the corporation was so controlled and manipulated that it had become a mere instrumentality of another." The plaintiff was unable to prove that the two corporations were not separate, and that recognizing two separate entities would sanction fraud or promote injustice.

AN IMPORTANT CHECKLIST

To determine whether two corporations are really separate and distinct, with neither accountable for the acts of the other, the courts generally look for the following:

✓ A lack of attention to corporate formalities
✓ Assets of the two corporations that are commingled
✓ Operations that are intertwined
✓ Evidence of complete domination and control by one
    corporation over the other

In another interesting case, a large conglomerate of family real estate businesses and multiple corporations was sued. The court found that the lines of control and responsibility were blurred among the many family businesses and inter-related corporations. For example, the various corporations had the same office, the same office staff, and the same directors and officers.

The court also found a great deal of financial intermingling between these companies. Funds were shifted from one account to another, and the corporations did not deal at arm's length with each other. The court ruled that the corporations weren't really separate and distinct, but rather acted in unison as one entity. The courts also stipulated that each entity was therefore responsible for the debts of the others.

In yet another case involving a personal injury action, the employee sued the corporation for which he worked, as well as the parent corporation. Although the parent corporation was involved in the day-to-day activities and operation of the subsidiary corporation, the court concluded that the parent did not dominate and control the subsidiary.

The court observed that the two corporations maintained separate books, records, bank accounts, offices, and staff, and that each consulted its own financial advisors, accountants, and stockbrokers. The court refused to pierce the corporate veil and hold the parent company liable for the judgment against the subsidiary corporation.

THE DANGERS OF OWNING AND USING BUSINESS ASSETS INCORRECTLY

While it is best to structure your business and assets correctly from the beginning, it is never too late to do so. As a matter of fact, one couple came to see me after they had unwittingly gotten into trouble with the U.S. government as well as with two state municipalities. They were facing multiple legal actions.

Although it appeared that this couple was coming to me too late, we carefully transferred their assets into limited partnerships. We knew that the transfers could possibly be found in violation of fraudulent conveyance laws, and thus unwound, but it would have been tragic in their innocent situation not to at least try to protect these assets.

I wasn't paid for my services, and I ended up writing off the bill. Eight years later, the couple appeared with checkbook in hand. "We've come to pay your bill," the husband announced. "We are grateful for what you did and are now in a position to pay you. Everything you did worked, and our house and other assets were saved by using the limited partnership." Needless to say, I was very pleased that things had worked out for this couple.

As a general rule, once a business finds itself in financial difficulties, it is too late to protect its assets. An insolvent business cannot dispose of its assets without receiving proper consideration and deprive its creditors of the collection of their debts. In general, if a creditor is awarded a judgment against a debtor, the creditor may go to the debtor's place of business with a sheriff armed with a levy and seize the assets.

Although it is tempting for the business owner to try to dispose of the corporate assets before they can be seized, consider the following case. A corporation agreed to remodel a home, then walked off the site when a conflict arose. The homeowner sued and was awarded over $60,000 in damages against the corporation. Meanwhile, the owner of the corporation depleted all of the assets of the corporation so that the homeowner wouldn't be able to get anything.

The court ruled that the corporation's owner was personally liable because he had wasted the corporation's assets. Because of this, the homeowner was able to collect from him personally. It is fairly routine in law that if a corporation's owner, director, or officer wastes or depletes the business assets, then the officers, directors, and even the shareholders can become personally liable.

Although I support using multiple entities for asset protection, I don't advocate doing it in an attempt to hide assets. In one case a corporation, in order to avoid a creditor, transferred all of its assets into a second corporation. This entity, in turn, transferred all of its assets to a third corporation. This series of maneuvers both looked and smelled like fraud, and the court disregarded all the transfers. Doing so allowed the judgment creditor to seize the assets regardless of their having been transferred to other entities.

Sometimes a failing corporation will sell company assets to family and friends for a minimal amount of money in order to evade a potential corporate creditor. In one case, property worth $25,000 was sold for $25. The court held that the transfer was fraudulent, and that it was an obvious attempt to get rid of the assets and make them unreachable by the corporation's creditor. The creditor was allowed to seize the assets anyway.

In another case, assets were transferred from a subsidiary corporation to its parent corporation in order to evade a judgment creditor. The court held that the creditor could seize assets from both the subsidiary corporation and its parent corporation.

BANKRUPTCY

When setting up a new business, anticipate and plan for what will happen if your business fails. The bankruptcy code states that the bankruptcy trustee may seize all of the debtor's nonexempt property, even if it is necessary to carry on the business. A corporation may be forced into bankruptcy, either voluntarily or involuntarily, and all of the assets of the corporation, including real estate, equipment, inventory, and accounts receivable may now be controlled by the trustee in bankruptcy. Begin with this condition in mind when you structure your business. Structure your business entities for maximum asset protection.

Now that you know the risks and advantages of using multiple entities, you must decide which structure is best for your businesses. Devise a checklist to help you pinpoint the compliance necessary to adhere to the rules and regulations governing those entities. Keep the entities as separate as possible. Your financial survival in today's world depends on it.

ACTION CHECKLIST

If you are setting up a new business, use different entities, whether corporations or partnerships, to insulate valuable assets from operations that are likely to be sued. If your business is already ongoing, it isn't too late. Go to an asset protection expert to discuss ways to transfer assets from existing corporations to a more protected structure. There are six good ways to do this:

1. Sell the assets to another entity from the corporation at a low but honest, fair market value, or

2. Distribute corporate assets as tax-deductible salary and wages to corporate officers

3. Make a list of all the real estate you presently own and how it is titled

4. Consider transferring real estate used by your business into a limited partnership or a limited liability company, or into your spouse's living trust or a children's trust

5. Decide which entity would best hold the real estate, and meet with your attorney to create the entity and transfer the real estate

6. Have a lease agreement drafted between your business and that entity, and scrupulously comply with all provisions of that lease agreement [1]

When the buzzards come after your hard-earned assets, it is too late!

When it comes to protecting your assets, there is no time like the present to begin looking at the "big picture." When you feel the *need* to do it, it is probably already too late.

---

1 Cover Your Assets: Lawsuit Protection, Jay W. Mitton, M.B.A., J.D. pgs. 171-188.

Do not get caught up in the procrastinating mindset that you can afford to wait until you have a few deals under your belt or until you make a certain amount of money. Every day you do not have adequate asset protection strategies in place, you are asking to be taken.

Many people who want what you have do not care about words like effort, labor, fruit, rewards, or for that matter words like honesty, integrity, truth, or justice. In fact, it may surprise you to know that there are many people who consider it their right to somehow have anything you do . . . whether they have earned it or not! They only care about getting as much as they can from whoever they can take it from. Do not let this be you.

Recognize that you have more than somebody else already, and they want what you have. Take the necessary steps to protect and preserve your assets now, so that as they grow, you and your family's financial future will be secure.

33

ACCOUNTING AND TAX SECRETS OF THE WEALTHY

◆

Although this is a very short chapter, it is one of the most essential considerations in this book. As unglamorous as they are, accounting and tax procedures have the potential of making you or breaking you. If stewarded properly, they will enhance your ability to accumulate wealth legitimately and permanently.

Just as structuring your real estate ownership to protect you from lawsuits is an important part of the millionaire mindset, so also is thoughtfully creating the most advantageous tax structure for your business. This is done, of course, to avoid paying unnecessary taxes, to eliminate certain taxes, or to postpone tax liability.

CORRECT ACCOUNTING PROCEDURES

In the area of business accounting, an ounce of prevention really *is* worth a pound of cure. Even if you are merely buying your first piece of property, get help in setting up the bookkeeping system necessary to monitor cash flow. There are several inexpensive computer software programs you can use, or you can merely keep track in a ledger. The point is, have a separate checking account for the project, and keep the income and expenses accounted for accurately. Also set up a file in which to keep your income and expense receipts. This way, when you purchase your next property, or increase the complexity of your real estate holdings, you will be able to more accurately forecast both income and expenses. Your projections and pro forma can be based on your actual experiences.

LIMITING TAX EXPOSURE

Many of the entity structuring techniques written about in previous liability protection chapters have direct impact on your overall tax picture. For example, with the proper structure, your business can provide you and your family with many "perks." These may include life insurance, health insurance, automobile and travel expenses, hotel costs, advertising costs, payroll for your spouse or children, and so forth. If you want to operate a business, take advantage of every option the federal government has provided to get and keep as much as you can from your labors.

The good news is that the government has recognized certain entity structures that deserve special tax breaks. For example, I encourage most of my clients to set up a "C" corporation as the managing entity for their real estate holdings. This strategy greatly increases their tax deductions. For example, Section 79 of the Internal Revenue Code allows tax deductions for life insurance. Section 105 allows deductions for family medical expenditures, such as saunas, swimming pools, and even penicillin pills. Section 162 and 212 allow travel expenses, even seminar and educational expense write-offs. As you can see, it is wise to consider forming a "C" corporation as you begin your business.

Remember, your primary objective is to *make* money. Keeping more of what you make (after taxes) is the same as making more.

As part of your millionaire mind-set, you do not want to leave your money sitting around doing nothing. As you remember, we mentioned in Section I that the key to ALL investing and business strategies is to turn each dollar as many times as possible each year so that your money is constantly making money.

Your goal is to pay the absolute legal minimum in taxes each year, and not one penny more. Would it surprise you to learn that this is all the IRS expects of you? Fortunately, as an investor there are certain very favorable tax structures — specific to real estate — that often eliminate taxes completely.

The greatest millionaire strategy is called tax-free exchanging. Yet probably ninety-five percent of real estate investors go about their business oblivious to deferred or simultaneous tax-free exchanges. A simple example will illustrate. Let's assume that you purchase a property for $10,000 and it is now worth $210,000. Normally you would pay taxes on the $200,000 gain. Millionaires learned long ago to avoid such taxes by simply trading their property for another property. Or, in a more advanced three-party transaction, you sell for cash your property to a buyer. You then have an attorney or some other intermediary hold your $210,000 until you have found a replacement property in which to invest it. As I said, the tax-free property exchange is often the greatest friend of the super wealthy.

The secret to successful tax planning for the real estate investor also includes the following considerations:

1. Always consider using a "C" corporation as your real estate management entity. This greatly increases your tax deductions and includes deductions you cannot have as an individual, or a LLC, or a partnership, or even an "S" corporation.

2. Have your tax advisors give you corporate resolutions under Sections 79, 105, 212, & 162 that will provide tax deductions for life insurance, medical, travel, vehicles, computers, phone systems, cell phones, pagers, staff support, furniture, paintings, swimming pool, sauna, and even health insurance premium payments.

3. When the time comes for selling a piece of real estate, use current tax law to reduce taxes on your gain. Use the tax-free exchange provisions, deferral provisions, and legal elimination provisions of tax law.

4. Consider spreading the income among more family members using the zero and low tax brackets of your relatives. The legal tools often used for this are Limited Partnerships, Limited Liability Companies, and "S" Corporations. Be wary of general partnerships because of your increased personal exposure. In fact, one absolute rule for my clients is: Never use a general partnership or an oral partnership.

To summarize, when you begin your real estate business, obtain professional advice and assistance. Set up a thorough accounting system. Once this is done, retain the services of a tax advisor. Minimizing taxes results in an increase of after-tax profits to you; and after all else is said, this is the name of the game.

34

PROPERTY MANAGEMENT AND LANDLORDING

———————— ◆ ————————

If you are going to rent properties anyway, why not get paid to manage them?

As an investor, one of the oldest practices in the profession is the renting of property. It is an essential part of buy and hold, as well as leases with options. As such, it is an excellent equity builder while waiting for markets to improve or inflation to increase your net worth.

"PROACTIVE" IS THE WORD

Renting property can be a headache, or it can be operated like a business. Anticipate, anticipate, anticipate! Proactively structure your rentals so that they require minimum maintenance. Do this so that the renters have the incentive to pay on time and so that damages and other problems are kept to a minimum. Plan to *not* do toilet repairs and other maintenance yourself, whether you have one rental unit or one hundred.

START TRAINING YOUR RENTERS AT THE BEGINNING

Establish a phone mailbox account and direct all calls to this account when advertising a rental. Establish a two-step message. First, describe the property details, including location and directions to get there. At this point, invite the inquirer to drive by and walk around it, making a visual inspection. After they have seen the house, have them progress to the second step, and leave their contact information. Speak with them when your schedule permits, rather than whenever they might have read the ad.

Set a time when you can progressively show the house to several people at once. By doing this, you will likely create a subtle "feeding frenzy," where people who would otherwise waste time sitting on a fence will make a decision.

During a "walk through," observe how the potential renters take care of themselves, their car, and their personal appearance. Trust any "yellow flags" you might see. If you feel good about a potential renter at this point, take a partial deposit fee to cover a background check. Next have them complete a credit application. If they are not accepted, their deposit money should be promptly returned. Make sure, in writing, that they understand the nonrefundable fee for processing the credit report. If they are reluctant to give you this processing fee, you are not required to consider them further.

Contract with a credit/skip trace service in your area to conduct a credit and background check. If the applicant has a criminal record or previous payment problems — especially with a previous rental — let them become someone else's problem, not yours.

Structure a lease agreement that gives the client a five percent incentive to pay before the first day of the month, a full rental amount until the fifth day of the month, and a percentage late fee after the fifth. Ask your advisor to talk with you about local requirements and restrictions on any of the contractual matters. You should always try to give your client the benefit of the doubt, but with your eyes wide open. Whenever possible, give them positive incentives first. Assess penalties only when incentives have not been effective.

Give good tenants incentives to extend their lease. I have heard it said that it can cost you four or five times more money to get a new tenant than it does to retain the one you presently have. It only stands to reason then that when you have a good tenant who is at the end of their lease, give them an incentive gift as an enticement to renew. Preferably, this can be something attached to the house, such as a ceiling fan, a bathroom update, repainting the interior or exterior, landscape work, etc. Their gift is actually an investment in the value of the property you may be planning on making anyway. Why not maximize its value and enhance loyalty at the same time?

Provide reliable maintenance. As you now understand fully, you are not in the contractor business. Establish a relationship with home repair and remodeling contractors, plumbers, electricians, appliance repair companies, heating and air conditioning contractors, etc.

Once you have established these contacts, you may want to consider the next level of involvement.Get paid to manage. There are undoubtedly many landlords in your area with one or two properties, who are tired of midnight phone calls about problems they have to deal with. Why not offer your services to them as well? For between five and ten percent of the gross rental amount, you can take on a number of accounts of this type. You may manage enough properties to warrant hiring a part-time manager to take care of the details. This assistant manager could assist your own rental clients as well as those you are now managing. I have noted, however, that once my client has twenty or more units, they should hire a professional management company to manage their properties. If you follow this rule of thumb, it will allow you to spend more of your valuable time finding more real estate deals.

FORMS FOR LANDLORDS

Once you have determined to spend part of your time as a landlord, simplify your tasks. Do this by setting up a file system that includes the necessary legal and/or management forms required to manage a tight rental ship. These forms could include:

✓ Rental application form
✓ Written instructions stating expectations for obtaining credit report and background check
✓ Rental unit preparation form
✓ Move-in checklist
✓ Maintenance request form
✓ Maintenance guarantee form
✓ Lease agreement, and
✓ Lease-option qualifying form

Though this is not an exhaustive list of forms needed to track your relationship with renters, it is a beginning. It will sensitize you to the need to "have things in writing." Renters have their own mentality, often without maintaining a sense of responsibility for their rental unit. By letting them know up front that you are organized and that you have a level of "inviolate expectations," you will tend to attract responsible renters. Whether you are interacting with them directly or through your manager, you must leave a paper trail of expectations and responsibilities.

The above-mentioned forms are available at your local office supply store or at a real estate rental agency. Your attorney may also have separate forms for your consideration. The point is, do business in writing. Being a "good ol' boy" on a handshake is the invitation to be taken advantage of. Remember, people (and therefore renters) either live up to, or down to, their perception of what others expect from them. This is human nature and provides the mandate for "forms and signatures."

PUTTING YOUR SYSTEM IN PLACE

If your time is limited, or if your investment strategy is to "buy and hold," learning the ropes of being a landlord is essential. If renting out your property provides reliable cash flow, and your end goal is to retain the property until you retire or until an ideal market arrives in which to sell, your wealth will appreciate accordingly. In addition, as your accountant or tax advisor can attest, expense deductions and depreciation may provide you with a tax-free income flow.

The point is, set up an accounting system that will allow you to maximize your profits, both while you own the property and then as you sell it.

35

MARKET TIMING AND CYCLES

───────◆───────

OF BULLS AND BEARS

When we use the term "market," most people think of the phrase, "stock market." Wall Street is an integral part of the overall economic market, but it may only distantly affect your personal market as a real estate investor. When the market is growing, inflation generally increases. There are often more jobs than there are qualified people to man them, and the economy is charging like a bull.

When the economy turns, deflation begins and interest rates often decrease. The job market tightens, and when this occurs the market is said to be lumbering and stumbling along like a bear.

SUPPLY AND DEMAND

In our economy, supply and demand slip along like the Oriental Yin and Yang. We have a free market system, which means that there are very few controls on our marketplace. Prices are generally "whatever the market will bear." Competition and other factors can affect the economy, but as a general rule, the major factors are supply and demand. In the short run, and as a general rule:

✓ As demand increases, supplies decrease

✓ As demand decreases, supplies increase

✓ When supplies are abundant, prices go down

✓ When supplies are few, prices go up

Whether the market is up or down, your real estate investment market is *always* up. Why is this the case? Because of the many strategies you have at your disposal. For example, often the best time to buy a wholesale "fixer-upper" house is when the economy is weak and new home purchases are down. What about when the market is strong and everybody is flush with cash? Who is looking at the ugly ducklings then? Supply is up, demand is down. A down market is therefore a good time for buying a wholesale house.

In a strong "high demand" market, there are many families who want to jump on the wagon and get into a home of their own. Even so, they often either cannot afford a new home, or their marginal credit will not permit them to. When the market is slow, people who can otherwise afford the new house often shy away from it. Instead, they look for the more modestly priced "used" retail house. While the specifics may change, you can have excellent money-making opportunities in both bull and bear markets.

In a down market, foreclosures go up. Because of this, if you are utilizing the strategies previously discussed, you will find some very good deals. When supplies go up, prices go down. During the recession of the 1990s, there were 10,000 new foreclosures a month in the Los Angeles area alone. You can imagine what that condition did to the prices at the auction block.

With some investment strategies, it is wise to switch and move between them depending on the marketplace. For example, undeveloped land can be a good buy in a bear market, but only if your exit strategy is not to attempt to immediately resell it. Buy and hold this property, or perhaps put one or more billboards on it. You may want to form a consortium to develop it when the market shows signs of improving. By putting storage units on the property, people who are "in foreclosure" in the down market can have a place to store their belongings when they move into an apartment.

As you understand and use the many different strategies available, you will learn to spot the opportunities when they are present, regardless of the market. From my perspective, this is what makes real estate America's greatest business opportunity.

BECOMING A STRATEGIC REAL ESTATE PLANNER

Prior to investing in real estate opportunities, the cautious investor will become a real estate strategist. A strategist is one who considers all variables before investing hard-earned money, time, and energy. As part of the strategy in real estate investing, it is essential to understand "market timing." That is, when is the right time to buy, and when is the right time to sell?

Real estate markets move through a cycle that typically takes seven to ten years to complete. This was the case throughout the United States in the 1990s. The market was just beginning to go into a downward spiral when the tragedy of September 11, 2001, transpired. The stock market collapsed, the federal interest rates were lowered, and the glut of real estate parcels in the marketplace quickly appeared. Prices dropped, unemployment increased, and our entire country went into recession alert. Long-term interest rates hit a thirty-year low, and home refinancing became vogue.

The intriguing thing that most people don't understand is the desirability of purchasing real estate while the market is struggling. More sellers are willing to carry contracts, prices are lowered, and banks are eager to solicit new clients for their lending portfolio and to unload REOs.

It is also good to purchase properties in a given market when the economy is on the rise. I was able to do this in the New York City market, purchasing several condominiums while my daughter and her husband were attending school there. Fortunately, we were able to sell these properties at a significant profit prior to the events of 2001.

While my wife and I had a specific strategy, and had become well-versed in the New York market, we were also recipients of a special gift. We got lucky. Part of real estate investing is being at the right place at the right time, with the right amount of dollars to invest. Even so, all other variables should be considered before investments are made.

Understanding the importance of market conditions when purchasing properties, one young client did what every investment newcomer hopes to do. He made an initial investment of less than $8,000 and leap-frogged to a fourteen-unit complex. He did this during a three-year period while the market was on the upswing. When he cashed out and invested in storage units, he had over $800,000 in net worth. Without making a mistake in market conditions, he was fortunate to begin his investment portfolio at the perfect time.

The nice thing about markets and market conditions is that they will always change. Markets seldom "flat line" and remain static. Money, time, and conditions blend together to produce sound, conservative investment opportunities. If you are able to determine when your market is going into its next growth mode, or how long you should hold properties you now own, you will be able to increase your wealth exponentially.

LESSONS FROM THE PAST

Looking back to a specific historical moment when the national economy was, in the main, very bad, will allow you to learn several key points in your investment strategy. When Jimmy Carter was president, interest rates for a single family home, owner occupied, with excellent credit, ranged from fifteen percent to seventeen percent, and this was on a first mortgage. Second mortgages soared as high as twenty-two percent. The economy was a mess.

Jump forward, if you will, into the next decade of the 1980s. Ronald Reagan was president, and in 1986, Congress passed a new Tax Act. This law penalized individuals who purchased real estate properties by reducing their tax write-offs. Many would-be real estate investors ceased buying real estate because of the adverse tax impact. In Dallas and Houston, Texas, large office buildings — even sky scrapers — sat empty and unoccupied. There was little tax incentive for promoters and syndicators to build.

The result of this trend was that an excess of "For Sale" properties appeared all over the country. Foreclosures and bank repossessions were everywhere. To help liquidate these properties, and to help the economy recover, the government set up what was called the Resolution Trust Corporation, or "RTC." The RTC seized over-extended savings and loan institutions, then proceeded to sell off the properties they had repossessed.

That was the down side. The upside was a plethora of "correctly priced" real estate parcels for sale. The wise investors bought up these properties, sometimes for pennies on the dollar. As an example, one client paid $152,000 for a property, when the real value of that property was $450,000. For the wise investor, it was the perfect environment in which to make sizeable returns on investment dollars.

MARKET MIGRATION

One of the key elements to market viability is what is called *economic migration*. This is the relocation of major corporations, as they take advantage of market lows. For example, Whirlpool relocated from New Jersey to Tulsa, Oklahoma. They did this in response to Tulsa economic conditions, which were influenced by oil prices. At that time, prices were down, the cost of living was depressed, and the cost of labor was low.

In response to these conditions, Tulsa city officials issued a directive that they would provide a tax abatement for any corporation that chose to relocate there. Whirlpool responded and was soon situated in Oklahoma. In reduced labor costs, alone, Whirlpool was able to save $250 million. They were also able to operate without incurring taxes. They employed several thousand employees, each of which created a "ripple effect" as the real estate market healed.

A Remarkable Success Story

One of my associates shares the following success story: "I purchased a twenty-four-unit apartment complex for $160,000. It was located in Kansas City, Missouri. At the time, economic conditions were deplorable. The purchase was made with this in mind, and almost immediately several large industrial giants relocated under the auspices of economic migration. One year later, I sold my property for $250,000. It was one of the best real estate investments I've participated in."

In summary, as one who is looking for the right market in which to invest, finding locations such as Tulsa or Kansas City allows you to buy real estate while it is at its lowest value. By holding this property for a year, or even two or three years, you are able to sell it in a healthy market. By this time, rents will have increased, vacancies will have dropped, and local unemployment will be at a minimum.

Many investors look for such conditions, and then they enter the real estate market with confidence and vision. Fortunes are made with every economic recession, and sophisticated investors are those who are able to maximize their profits by following these trends.

36

ANTICIPATING AND SPOTTING TRENDS

◆

STAYING ON THE CREST OF THE WAVE

Spotting trends involves cerebral activity and intuition. When you understand that progress moves in waves, and that there are usually signs of what is to come, the trick is to look around you and absorb what you see. You can use the following checklist:

✓ Look at a plat map of your county or an aerial photograph of an area. Where are the blank areas without streets or houses? Opportunity knocks.

✓ How many new building permits are being submitted? Is there an area of your town that is coming back after a long decline?

✓ Where are people moving? What are income levels in the different areas around you?

✓ What area of town does not have adequate shopping, recreational facilities, storage or business space?

✓ Where are new roads planned?

The following are specific tasks for you to consider. Take proactive steps as well:

✓ Attend zoning commission meetings

✓ Research the city planner's long-range plans

✓ Ask your local councilman or alderman, "Where is the growth going to be?"

✓ Look at land records for undeveloped land. Often you will find a few individuals or groups in your community owning several blocks of land

✓ Review local university economic studies of land use and pro formas

What would you have done twenty years ago if you had realized that waterfront was going to go from mosquito-infested, low-rent housing to multimillion dollar estates? When developers began building large-scale apartment complexes in the eighties, did you think they were crazy? That is okay. I thought the same thing the first time I saw a storage unit. Opportunity knocks to those who understand and who have vision.

In summary, there is no magic crystal ball involved in the real estate investment process. Armed with what you know about your area, and what you now understand about the strategies in real estate, ask yourself key questions. Then act on the answers. By doing so, you will be on the crest of the wave, rather than being crushed by it or just watching it pass you by.

WHAT MAKES REAL ESTATE THE GREATEST BUSINESS FOR *YOU?*

———————◆———————

WHY REAL ESTATE?

For over thirty-five years as a practicing attorney, I have worked with many multimillionaire (and even some billionaire) clients. While strategizing with these extraordinarily wealthy individuals, I have been amazed to discover that all of them, except one, made their fortunes in real estate. The one exception actually created his wealth in the stock market.

For one client, wealth may have been created through the buying and selling of single family homes. For another, commercial property. Still another, dealing in "paper," tax liens, or rental properties. Whenever I probed into their background, the answer was always the same: real estate. I was their attorney, their "hired hand" when it came to legal matters, and I was honored to be so.

As attorney to these millionaires, I was privy to the most intimate financial details of their lives and businesses. I began to see the "behind the scenes" methods these wealthy individuals used. I spoke at length with them and their advisors about their finances, their deals, their cash-

flow and investments, their long- and short-term goals. I
learned how they got where they are today, and how they
planned to reach their future goals.

These clients shared their wealth-creating secrets with
me and literally mentored me. Frankly, their "secrets"
weren't really all that secret, until you realize that these are
the types of things spoken of over dinner or in private. In
essence, they freely shared their favorite techniques and
areas of focus.

There have been many seminar speakers who have
taught real estate investing, who learned by experience. In
their own life they took a little knowledge and a lot of grit
and determination, and beat their way through the
University of Hard Knocks to build a successful real estate
business. This is commendable. It is also somewhat
misleading and comes with a caution:

We are each unique in talent and expertise. I strongly
urge you to focus your buying on *one* of the twenty-one
"cookie cutter" approaches in Section II. Get some
experience. Simultaneously, get educated. Attend classes or
seminars. While you are doing these two things, find a
mentor. This is the ultimate weapon. If you can find a
mentor you can trust, he or she will change your life forever.
My mentors have done this for me, teaching me more than
I could have ever learned in the classroom.

**"So, why is real estate the greatest business for *me*, and
how do I fit it to my circumstances?"**

For one thing, real estate really does not depend on
your current economic circumstances. You can control the
buying and selling of property without using a dime of your
own money. Compare this to the stock market where the

phrase, "It takes money to make money" originated. To buy and sell stocks usually takes liquid assets.

With real estate, however, you not only do not need money to make money. You can often actually build a better business if you do not use all your own money. There are many ways to use the seller's money, your buyer's money, other people's money, and even the equity in the house. There are ways to defer, reduce, and even eliminate down payments completely. You simply do not need to use your own cash to structure a deal. There are no franchise fees, inventory costs, or other "normal" start-up costs with this business. You can begin immediately, and work to achieve your financial dreams.

Fast return. Many business plans reach out two, three, five years or more to show a return on investment. In real estate, your return can come at closing, in a matter of a few weeks or months, and keep on coming. If making cash fast is a part of what you are looking for, real estate may hold the answer.

Long-term, diversified income. While "fast" is good, if you are looking for more long-term plans, real estate is here to stay. Generally speaking, the good news is that real estate usually increases in value from year to year. Even if your long-term holdings do not appreciate every year, your income can still climb. I know of no other business where these dynamics work to allow you to benefit so effectively.

No license required. I do not know why some people have the "license required" notion stuck in their mind, but there is not one state in the country that requires you to have a license to buy and sell real estate. If this were true, you would have to get a license to buy your own home or sell it yourself. The only license requirements for a real estate investor buying and selling property may be a driver's license. If you want to make serious money, be an investor. No license is required and you almost always pay lower taxes.

No degree is required. This means not even a high school diploma. Many people are accustomed to seeing ads that say, "degree required," or feel lacking because they do not have a college degree. You should not be surprised to learn that many of my multimillionaire clients are college dropouts. In fact, some even failed to complete high school.

Familiar turf. Real estate is all around us — houses, apartments, and office buildings. Unlike intangibles such as stocks, bonds, and commodities, real estate is *real*. As you know, real estate is tangible. You can see it and touch it. You do not need to be a rocket scientist to understand the concepts or to make money in real estate.

When you first started out, did you obtain a loan when you purchased your automobile? As you know, the process is the same when buying a house. In both cases, you have papers to sign. As I'm sure you know, with a house this paper-signing ceremony is called the "closing." When you pay off the loan on your car or your house, you keep your car or home. The only difference is that the house is likely worth a lot more than when you bought it, while the car is worth much less.

Good alternative income. You are secure in your company, your career, your position, your community. You might cringe at the prospect of going into a multi-level business, or a vending machine franchise. There are many good reasons multimillionaires choose real estate. Real estate is observable and respectable. It can inject large sums of cash into your estate. You can increase the effectiveness of your financial plans with the boost coming from the added cash-stream real estate can provide.

Land on your feet. In today's world, downsizing is a way of life. You can make sure you are never again so dependent upon a job that you risk having the rug pulled out from under you. You do this by building a future in real estate. Because you do not have to tap your savings or unemployment to build it, maybe it is just what the doctor ordered.

Have it your way. Whether you are an extrovert or introvert, mechanically inclined or a klutz, you can design your real estate business to fit *you*. It can fit your personality, the demands of your life, your likes and your dislikes.

Family business. You and your partner can each handle different parts of the business and build it together. You can even involve your children, helping them get their first investment properties. While many businesses separate family members, real estate involvement has the potential of bringing them together.

Single's scene. While you are building a secure future, you are also meeting good, new people. You are setting your own schedule and building your future on your own terms. It gives you an incredible sense of control and fulfillment because it is a business you can build on your own.

Just starting out. If you are in your late teens or early twenties and just getting your career rolling, you can structure real estate around your job demands and still take control of your future. Even with only a modest number of deals in a year, you can easily surpass your current income. You can build a second career that will change your financial picture for the rest of your life.

Ready to retire. Now you are in my age group. If you are a senior or middle aged, your expectations of retirement likely do not include working at the grocery store to make ends meet. There are so many ways you can enjoy your retirement with the extra money from just a few real estate deals each year. And, you've worked hard long enough so you deserve to enjoy your retirement

See the USA. As an investor, you can legally and easily buy and sell property in all fifty states. Make real estate a simple part of your trips. Look at and make offers on properties, and the Internal Revenue Service will even help pay for your travels. They do this under Section 162 and 212 of the IRS Code. When you visit the grandchildren, buy a house. If you find some area you just love and want to return to again and again, buy property when you go there, and once again the IRS will help out.

Or, stay put and do only as much as you want to do from your home. Real estate can fit into one, two, three hours a week — or it can consume every day of the week. It is up to you. You can earn as much or as little as you want, and live your retirement to the max on your own terms.

Like me, you may be planning to serve your church or community. It's nice to earn while you serve others. Or, this may be the time for you to finally learn to paint, to play the piano, or to volunteer your time to a local charity. Whatever your retirement dreams are, real estate can fit right in, helping to fund your plans on your own terms.

You are in control of your life. The most significant advantage I saw in real estate was that I could accomplish what I wanted, on my own schedule. It was not like so many businesses that turned into just another job I couldn't get away from. With real estate, it is not how much or how little you work at it. Rather, it is how consistent you keep the pace you set for yourself. Of course, we all can use a little help keeping focused and on target. Finding a good mentor can help keep you focused and accelerate your learning process.

It does not matter if you are working at a dead-end job or making just over minimum wage. Nor does it matter if you are a successful CEO who is tired of burning the candle at both ends. You may be reading this as a single mom, trying to hold your family together. Or, you may be a retiree who has the luxury of traveling the country, but is always looking over his shoulder at the stock market's numbers or the increasing costs of medications. You could be a tradesman, working for years in your craft, knowing that your physical body can only keep going so long. Or, you may be a recent graduate bumping into the "experience required" ads over and over again, wanting to make your own way.

Whoever you are, real estate investments can give you the extra *oomph!* you need in your life.

Wise real estate investments can give you money, time, and security. Real estate can give you extra income, replace your income, replace your spouse's income, balance out your investment portfolio, or give you the extra you need to cover college tuition.

For some, it means a lifetime of financial independence: Income that keeps coming in month after month, whether you do anything new or not. As one of my clients put it, "I finally realized I could not shut off the income once I had it going!"

Let me now invite you to put this book down and

simply begin. Don't procrastinate. By taking one step at a time, you will financially bless your family for the rest of your lives. Hopefully, like myself, you will be fortunate in finding a mentor. As I have expressed throughout this book, I am grateful to the millionaire clients who were my special mentors. With my family, I owe a debt of gratitude to them. I wish you remarkable success along your road to untold wealth.

12/17   4pm
1/7   GUITAR
1/28   Lesson
          DATES